METALLICA

THE COMPLETE ILLUSTRATED HISTORY

MARTIN POPOFF

With

RICHARD BIENSTOCK

DANIEL BUKSZPAN

NEIL DANIELS

ANDREW EARLES

KEVIN ESTRADA

GARY GRAFF

WILLIAM HALE

BOB LEAFE

JAAN UHELSZKI

MICK WALL

FRANK WHITE

VOYAGEUR
PRESS

CONTENTS

INTRODUCTION

> "The guys in the band are genuinely—
> and quite incredibly, given their
> crazy lives—likeable dudes"

First off, I must express how much of a challenge it is writing a book this "concise" on Metallica, wishing I could go on and on into a six-figure word count. No, the idea with the trunk of this book is to provide the story of the band using a level of detail that doesn't overpower Elements II and III of this headbanged trip, namely, the reviews of the band's catalog by top music journos and them yummy visuals.

To my mind, these components are equally important to the band's narrative, and in fact the book that will most satisfy the fan who fancies himself any sort of expert on Lars & Co. You'll laugh, you'll cry, you'll hurl, as our army of strong-minded smarty pants rave on about records that range from towering classics to mediocre to wildly controversial. I mean, sure, there have been many fine books and other sources—the 'net, film documentaries, DVDs—from which to learn the band's history, but this heavy, heavy writing . . . it's all new and it's all bloody interesting.

And then there are the visuals, the good doctor Dennis Pernu and Voyageur Press continuing to do this series of books proud (seek them out) by assembling a feast for the eyes. Bottom line, the book you hold in your hands is the bestest place to peruse Metallica—all the bits and pieces and a bunch of fine photography in a perfect balance further steadied by the visuals' relationship to our two types of text.

Now lemme just tell you how the magic of Metallica has affected me personally. First off, the guys in the band are genuinely—and quite incredibly, given their crazy lives—likeable dudes. And even more significant than their disarming nature on me personally, they are all essentially my age and got into metal for the exact same reason that I did, or any of my buddies (like Brian Slagel for instance) who wound up something other than players. That's obviously not to say I can compare my accomplishments or lot in life to any of those guys—I'm just some idiot. Just sayin' this because there's a weird commonality of experience, especially with Lars (and Slagel), that makes us and a bunch of our mutual acquaintances part of an easyspeak tribe, sorta fans first, with everything else we get to do in the industry just gravy.

Don't want to ramble much more, but I just want to mention both my first and second impressions of Metallica, and then we will be off like metal militia with whiplash. Snap yer neck like Newsted (ouch) back to 1983. No, I was not a tape trader, but I did know bloody everything about the New Wave of British Heavy Metal (NWOBHM) and, for that matter, every metal record on the planet (the full-length ones, anyway).

Then *Kill 'Em All* arrived. I can remember it like it was yesterday. Like I said, these guys were basically us, but they got to make a record. And they got to use all that "this week and last week in metal" knowledge that we would also use to make up songs (or mostly riffs for songs) in our own professional bar band, the mighty Torque, for one summer. All too evident to anybody inside this music, *Kill 'Em All* was straight to the point, the kind of thing a NWOBHM fan might make if he wanted

to kick that music's ass, make it nastier, find better riffs than any on *Angel Witch* or *The Nightcomers*. But at the same time, *Kill 'Em All* was not my favorite album—it just seemed too soiled, nasty, street-level, barked into the mic, and . . . I dunno, rigid and obsessed with the riff at the expense of everything else. Still, it was most definitely *way* up the lists of great albums of 1983 that we would churn out while sitting at my buddy Fiver's kitchen table while the Bose 901s blasted in the living room, powered by Yamaha's monster 160-watts-per-channel CR-3020 receiver, all eighty-two pounds of it wrapped in teak.

Flash forward to 1984. (This story has been in some of my previous books and, alas, I got the facts a bit wrong. Here it is fixed, thanks to a recently located notebook in which I recorded all my record purchases.) On June 17, I had gotten back from Spokane, Washington, with Savatage's *Sirens* ($7.99 at Strawberry Jams) and Savage's *Loose 'n Lethal* ($8.99 at Mirage) and was just beside myself with how the latter was one of the greatest albums ever made and the former had quite possibly just taken over actual top spot (my favorite part of this whole damn book is having Jonny Z tell me they almost recorded *Ride the Lightning* at Par Studios in Florida, where Savatage got such a massive sound).

I always needed a quiet lie-down whenever the best album list got a new No. 1, but this time there would be no rest because on August 3 I got *Ride the Lightning*, the U.K. issue, for $14.39 at Lyle's Place in Victoria, British Columbia. Savatage was whacked, ending the shortest reign at No. 1 ever. I remember putting the needle down on "Fight Fire with Fire" and . . . the inhumanity. This was clearly music made by immortals, the greatest song ever. You could barely even process how James and Kirk could play that. The rest was almost as good, especially the title track and "For Whom the Bell Tolls," which, if you're sitting on the edge of your bed and the first three songs in a row are that good . . . I was just losing my mind. This had only happened with me an' my buddies twice before: Priest's *Sad Wings of Destiny* and *Stained Class*, and the next time would be Mercyful Fate's *Melissa* (which, I'm just surprised to see, I only got three months after *Ride the Lightning,* same day as that Danish quint's *Don't Break the Oath*—October 26, A&B Sound, $5.88 and $6.99, respectively).

Anyway, that's it. Thanks for indulging me that trip down Headbanger Alley, all to illustrate how upsetting of the apple cart James, Lars, Kirk, and Cliff were to my metal world, and that's without even getting into how *Master of Puppets* outright won the endless polling I conducted to write my book *The Top 500 Heavy Metal Albums of All Time*. Of course, then all the vehement debating begins, the daggers come out, and we talk about the weird production on *Justice*, the lack of thrash on *Metallica*, and on and on to what is the kick-ass last and current studio album of the journey, *Death Magnetic*, and the subsequent novel ways these sociable four guys brought that record—along with their massive metal-moving hits—to the fans in the seven years since.

So look, learn, read on. Hope you have as much fun digesting this book as I did writing it, 'cause, as I say, the whole process felt like . . . well, like sitting around the kitchen table with Lars, Fiver, Nalbandian, Metal Tim, Slagel and James, making up lists.

Martin Popoff
martinp@inforamp.net
www.martinpopoff.com

All www.WycoVintage.com

The Old Waldorf, San Francisco, October 18, 1982. The band would soon grow dissatisfied with McGovney's bass chops and bring in Trauma's Cliff Burton. © Bill Hale

1.
A DANGEROUS MEETING

1981–1982

"The English bands were more about playing what they wanted and, 'F*** you, we don't care about record contracts; we'll just put it out ourselves.' This was obviously borrowed directly from the punk thing. It was metal getting a second wind from the streets. That is where the thrash and speed bands in the '80s got their attitudes from. It wasn't what you looked like; it was like, here's the music, here's the attitude, and we don't give a f*** what anybody else thinks about it." —Lars Ulrich, *US Rocker*, 1991

Somewhere between *Unleashed in the East* and *British Steel*, Judas Priest had moved heavy metal from a kerranging, mathematical guitar sound used often enough on records to pass muster, toward a language, a package, a credo, a multisensory experience. A light bulb flashed with the kids and an often-denigrated music became a badge (or sew-on patch) of honor. The New Wave of British Heavy Metal turned Priest's whistling in the dark into an army screaming for vengeance—vengeance upon the punks, upon peaceful easy country rock, upon disco, upon glam.

Ron McGovney at the Stone, San Francisco, September 18, 1982.
© Bill Hale

Glam? Well, Ol' Blighty's version of it circa Sweet, Mott, and Slade didn't need much extra killing, but thousands of miles away, in music-confused Los Angeles, this new heavy metal that headbangers could call their own . . . well, it was threatening to go the way of the hairspray. Good guitarists, sure, but why so pretty?

One surmises that most of the new peacock gang took much from the couple of dozen exciting new and unapologetic NWOBHM bands, but none were so struck by Motörhead, Saxon, Tygers of Pan Tang, Angel Witch, Holocaust, Fist, Raven, Tank, and Venom as a skinny young fan of exotic Danish tennis-themed origin known as Lars Ulrich. And "fan" is the operative. This guy wasn't even a drummer yet, but that didn't stop him from getting a record deal, for which he would soon need to learn drums and build a band of rascals to play the part of. . . . Well, their name would have to suggest "encyclopedia," with the further implication that if you looked up "heavy metal" in a dictionary, there'd be a little line drawing of Metallica.

The record deal was just a dumb dream with Ulrich's equally goofy buddy, Brian Slagel, soon to be bossman of Metal Blade Records and still head headbanger three decades later. "Before I started working in the record store, trying to follow the New Wave of British Heavy Metal was somewhat difficult, being in L.A.," Slagel recalls. "Some of the stuff would kind of trickle in and then of course I met Lars at a Michael Schenker concert in L.A. He was wearing the Saxon European T-shirt and I thought, 'What the hell is that?' So we started going around the record stores. And it was me and my friend John Kornarens and Lars, and we were the only three people in L.A. that even knew the NWOBHM existed. And there weren't very many record stores that had stuff. So we would drive, like two, two and a half hours and there's three of us, and there were three singles or whatever we were trying to find."

"But it was cool meeting him, because he had a lot of stuff that we didn't have, and vice versa. . . . At that point, you're so cut off being in L.A. The scene was happening six thousand miles away and you're just desperate for any morsel of information on anything. And this was so difficult to get. It was obviously long before the Internet. So it was cool because, wow, there's another guy who's into the same stuff we're into. So I would say probably about once every two weeks we would go out on a record-finding mission. We would be grilling the sales clerks: 'OK, we gotta get this, we gotta get that, can you order that?'"

The Stone, San Francisco, September 18, 1982. © Bill Hale

The Old Waldorf, San Francisco, October 18, 1982. *All © Bill Hale*

14

Long story short, Slagel began working at Oz Records and bringing the damn records in himself, Iron Maiden's debut making a huge impact. He even started his own U.K.-style 'zine, *The New Heavy Metal Revue*.

"So I was thinking about the big *Metal for Muthas* compilation and I thought, maybe I'll do one here," Slagel continues. "So I called all the big distributors and record stores and said, 'If I put a compilation together of all the L.A. heavy metal bands, would you guys sell it?' and they said sure. So I just went around to all the bands and said, 'Hey, if you guys have a demo track, I'm going to put together a compilation album in conjunction with the magazine.' I just said, 'Just give me a track and I'll put it on there,' and everybody said, 'OK, fine.' And then Lars called me up one day and said, 'Hey, can I be on your album if I put together a band?' And I said, 'Sure, why not?' And that's how the whole Metallica thing started. He started to jam with people. We were over at his house one time. You know, Lars was this crazy little sixteen-, seventeen-year-old Danish kid who was just all over the place and we would park the car, and before the engine was turned off, Lars was out of the car and in the record store. So we were running after him, 'He's going to get all the singles!' So we were over at his house one time and

"If I put a compilation together of all the L.A. heavy metal bands, would you guys sell it?"

—Brian Slagel

there was the drum set sitting in the corner, not even put together and he was saying, 'I'm going to start a band.' 'Yeah, sure you are Lars, right.' And he started jamming with James."

Slagel continues: "When he was over in Denmark, he had started to play a little bit," referring to Lars' move to L.A. with his crazy, creative post-hippie family in 1980. "We had known him for a while and the drum set was just sitting in the corner of his room not put together. He finally did put it together. He went to England. He went over there before John [Kornarens] and I did, and he hung around in the scene, met all the bands, got influenced to start something. So he came back, put together his drum set, and started jamming. But he didn't have anybody to jam with, so he put some ads in the paper. Him and Hetfield jammed a bit, but nothing happened. And then Lars, the ever-scheming guy he is, when I was doing the record, he thought, 'Well, this is a perfect opportunity. I'll call James and say, "Hey, we can be on a record so let's keep jamming."' So that's pretty much what happened."

Lars did indeed get fired up by the NWOBHM firsthand, having made the pilgrimage to England, where he tagged along with the great Diamond Head, soaking up a ton of influences. Back home, his want ad in *Recycler* had read, "Drummer looking for other musicians to jam with Tygers of Pan Tang, Diamond Head, and Iron Maiden," exotic code words designed to weed out those not tapped in, as well as those who were too pretty.

"I was growing up in L.A., where glam was king," explains James Hetfield, then rhythm guitarist and vocalist in this duo auditioning prospective members. "I would say queen—glam was queen [laughs]. You know, that was live rock. If you wanted to go see a band, the heaviest you could see—unless Motörhead or somebody was coming through that was imported [laughs]—you were looking at Ratt or Mötley Crüe. And there were hundreds and hundreds and hundreds of those bands. We weren't necessarily hanging out with those guys, at all. Obviously there was Brian Slagel, who was in touch with the heavier side of things in the L.A. area, but we were not hanging out. I mean, there were times where we would go and

hang and watch a band like Ratt or something, and just go, 'Wow, they've got a lot of gear,' you know [laughs]. 'I want that!' But that was pretty much it. But you know, they influenced us a lot, in the sense that we don't want to do that. They inspired us with . . . anger."

Hetfield had much reason to be angry, the preposterousness of hair metal aside. He had come from a broken home, his strict Christian Scientist parents divorcing in 1976 when he was thirteen years old. Three years later, his mother died of cancer, refusing treatment, per her religious beliefs. Conversely, Ulrich was raised in relative comfort, his father Torben being a known tennis pro and a bit of a renaissance man. The younger Ulrich had seriously excelled in tennis, as well, before being bitten by the music bug after his father took him to a Deep Purple concert in Copenhagen before their move to the States.

Prior to jamming with Ulrich, Hetfield recalls he "was learning about some of the more established harder rock bands, like Scorpions or Priest. I was so young, I wasn't going to gigs anyway. So I wasn't really hanging out. I just remember, obviously at school, there was punk rock and heavy metal. I don't remember really seeing any glam kids at our school. I liked some punk. I discovered the Ramones and AC/DC kind of the same time. It was one of those things. It's like, everyone is thinking, 'Why have you got them in the same . . . you know, they're touching each other in your record collection! Arrrghhh!' So what? They've got raw energy, man. That was it. Same with Motörhead. Obviously the punks were hanging out at Motörhead shows, and headbangers were going to some of the early punk shows. As far as the glam thing, that was pretty much the ugly sister of music at that point [laughs]. You were either in it or you were not."

Metallica's lineup had evolved from Ulrich and Hetfield with Lloyd Grant, to a four-piece consisting of Ulrich and Hetfield, Ron McGovney on bass, and one Dave Mustaine on lead guitar and heavy attitude. Mustaine had much in common with Hetfield, and even more anger, having grown up in a family of Jehovah's Witnesses ruled over by a violent, alcoholic father. By seventeen he was off

The Old Waldorf, San Francisco,
November 29, 1982. © Bill Hale

"Anybody with any taste who liked metal— long before there was thrash, and when thrash kicked in—L.A. wasn't the place,"

—Ron Quintana

his leash, dealing drugs, doing drugs, and dreaming of turning his guitar playing into a vocation in the tradition of his hard rock heroes, AC/DC, Judas Priest, KISS, and Black Sabbath.

The new band's ill fit in L.A. was so pronounced that they would eventually move to San Francisco and quickly became the focal point—along with Exodus—of a scene that could be called the birth of thrash, depending, that is, on how one defines Motörhead, Venom, Tank, Raven, and Canada's Anvil. "In the early '80s, San Francisco was really punk rock," explains Chuck Billy of Testament, Frisco's second-most famous thrash act, describing a scene based at clubs such as Ruthie's Inn, The Stone, and Mabuhay Gardens. "And then Metallica arrived to the Bay Area. We had Exodus and stuff like that, but when Metallica arrived, for us in the Bay Area, it was such a young, hard, new, aggressive sound that we loved. And we also loved the fact that Metallica wasn't going to try to get videos or radio. They were just going to go on the raw power of the music. So I think all of us, the Bay Area

None of the hairspray bands in early-1980s L.A. were so struck by Motörhead, Saxon, Tygers of Pan Tang, Angel Witch, Holocaust, Fist, Raven, Tank, and Venom as a skinny young fan of Danish origin known as Lars Ulrich.

bands, were wanting that. But fortunately for the Bay Area, we didn't just copy that. Each band that came out of the Bay Area—Exodus, Testament, Death Angel, Forbidden, Vio-lence—all these bands that were thrash bands in the '80s had their own sound. We didn't all just try to copy Metallica. But we were really inspired by their attitude and what they stood for."

"For me, it was James Hetfield," continues Billy, asked about his key inspirations, particularly as a vocalist. "Totally. A combination of power and melody. Before I joined the band, I went to school and college and tried to be a vocalist, where it was all about trying to be melodic, to have melody. And then when I got turned onto Metallica, Exodus, all of that, the whole style changed from not just being melodic through the whole thing, but having power with melody. So for me, that was right up my alley. . . . I wanted to sing more aggressively, but I wanted to have a hook and carry a tune, the whole bit."

"Everyone hated L.A.," adds Ron Quintana, who came up with the name Metallica. Quintana and Ulrich had been pondering whether he should call his new fanzine *Metallica* or *Metal Mania*. Ulrich helpfully steered him toward the latter, snagging the authoritative "measuring stick" tag for himself. "Anybody with any taste who liked metal—long before there was thrash, and when thrash kicked in—L.A. wasn't the place," Quintana continues. "But, you know, L.A. is a big place. There's plenty of room for posers *and* for metalheads. But San Francisco's always been more hardcore than L.A. . . . There was a big hardcore scene in L.A., but it took them a while to make the transition to the crossover of punk/metal, which is almost what thrash is. L.A., that's where all the bands went to get label-signed and stuff. San Francisco has always had that problem. We always lost good bands to L.A. Metallica was one of the few to reverse that trend [laughs]."

Metal Mania would feature Metallica's very first spot of press, Bob Nalbandian and Patrick Scott sending in a report from L.A. that pronounced Lars & Co. "The heaviest of all LAHM bands!!! Originally founded in May 1981 by local HM madman Lars Ulrich, this five-piece has accomplished quite a lot in the three months the present lineup has been together. Metallica's first break was when they were invited to record their potential classic 'Hit the Lights' on the forthcoming compilation *Metal Massacre* album, which features LA HM bands. After much local destruction, they supported Saxon in LA and will soon support Krokus at their two LA shows. On stage, Metallica, known as the 'Young Metal Attack,' come across as a British-type headbanging band and their songs, like 'Metal Militia,' 'Jump in the Fire,' 'Motorbreath' and 'The Mechanix' are all fast and ultra-heavy! Watch out for this band; they have the potential to become US HM Gods! They are currently trying to get a deal with an independent LA label for a vinyl release by this summer."

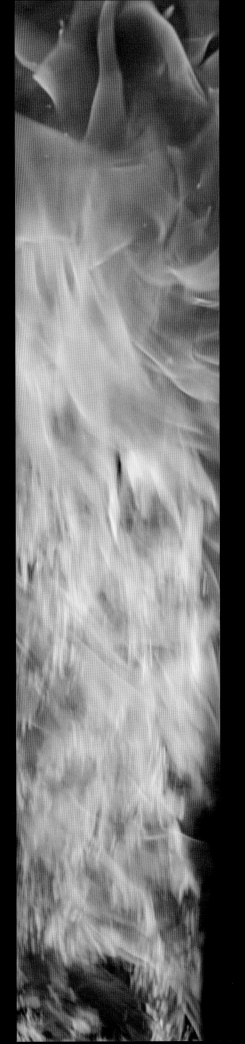

As they ascended through the ranks, Metallica had recorded one demo (needed to land a gig—this one is known as *Power Metal*), and then another featuring "Jump in the Fire," "The Mechanix," "Motorbreath," and "Hit the Lights," the latter of which did indeed wind up on Slagel's historic and seminal *Metal Massacre* compilation—a first attempt on the first pressing, a second version on the second pressing.

"I had four bands in total that I was liaison with," recalls John Kornarens, on the assembly of the sampler. "Brian had four himself—like Bitch, Cirith Ungol, Ratt—and I had Metallica, Malice, Steeler, and Avatar. So we took care of it and they all got us tapes—except for Lars. Basically we had all the tapes, we had to go down to the Bijou studio in Hollywood, we had time booked to do the album, to actually put everything in the right format,

and [get it] mastered. And Lars was supposed to meet us at three o'clock when our sessions started with the final version of 'Hit the Lights.' I had heard a rough version of it. At three o'clock we met on the sidewalk and I guess there was a mixup between Lars and Brian because Lars thought that Brian was going to pay for the fifty-dollar mastering [fee] and Brian thought Lars was bringing fifty bucks for the mastering fee. And of course Lars didn't have fifty bucks and Brian didn't have fifty bucks, so Lars looked at me and said, 'Do you have fifty bucks?' And I had fifty-two dollars in my wallet, so I pulled out fifty bucks and said, 'Here.' And he said, 'I'll pay you back; I promise,' which he did. And that's how Metallica got on *Metal Massacre*."

The Hetfield/Ulrich/Mustaine/McGovney lineup was also responsible for the band's third and much-lauded

LIGHTNING TO THE NATIONS

Lars was fired up by the NWOBHM, and even made a pilgrimage to England, where he tagged along with the great Diamond Head.

"Brian thought Lars was bringing fifty bucks for the mastering fee. And of course Lars didn't have fifty bucks so Lars looked at me and said, 'Do you have fifty bucks?'"

—John Kornarens

No Life 'til Leather demo of July 1982, which consisted of "Hit the Lights," "The Mechanix," "Motorbreath," "Seek & Destroy," "Metal Militia," "Jump in the Fire," and "Phantom Lord." It was enough material and potent enough to put the band at the vanguard of a nastier, more riff-insistent, and even faster form of "speed metal" to the point where the style of metal at hand was renamed. The term "thrash" made sense to all involved, namely the band and their circle of friends, all budding journalists and photographers documenting the scene.

Bob Nalbandian, now writing for his own metal 'zine, *The Headbanger*, sagely wrote, "I must admit that this was one of the heaviest demo tapes I've ever heard!!! After hearing their tape, I found it hard to believe that the band are actually from the US. The band's present lineup has been together for some three months and have opened for such HM greats as Saxon. Metallica has what it takes to be a HM band. They are all young and very ambitious and most importantly they're experienced scholars in the HM field. Their musicianship is also of high standard, most notably Dave Mustaine's ultrafast guitar work. I think that the band will soon make the English HM scene think differently about American metal and will soon be in competition with many of the NWOBHM bands."

Asked if Ulrich was more about taking care of business or the music itself, thrash expert and journalist John Strednansky muses, "Both, but it started with the music. He used to call me at my house, or from rehearsals, and put the phone down and say, 'You gotta hear this new song that I heard.' Or he would call me and talk to me about Accept when 'Fast as a Shark' came out. The first time I ever heard that song was when Lars played it to me over the phone. He used to tell me about all these new singles from England that came out, and actually when he was hurting financially . . . he sold his record collection. Well, I was the one who bought those. So with him it was totally about the music early on. And then he realized, hey,

I know I'm going to be huge doing this. And that came early on. But I think the original impetus was his love of the music—he turned his tennis career down for the music."

"He always looked like a natural [on drums]," Strednansky continues. "He looked great. He was into it and I used to bring him water in the early days when he was playing [laughs]. He just never let up. He just never, ever let up. And that's what blew me away—he was driven. He probably could've played a five-hour gig in those days."

> ## "Lars had a little playbook, a step-by-step of what he did. He had a sense, that rock 'n' roll sensibility or something in there that, okay, this is going to be huge."
> ### —Bill Hale

But the rest of the rhythm section was a problem. In late 1982 Ron McGovney was replaced by Trauma's Cliff Burton, who famously wouldn't join unless the band raised stakes and moved to San Francisco, which they did, specifically to El Cerrito across the bay.

"Trauma was on *Metal Massacre II*, and they were from San Francisco," explains Slagel. "They had this crazy manager and stuff and they had sent us the demo tape… and we thought, let's have them on *Metal Massacre* and we brought them down to L.A. for a *Metal Massacre* show. I saw the band and they were pretty good, but the bass player was just incredible. I thought, 'Oh my God, this bass player is just awesome!' And by that time Metallica had started. They were doing the demo and had started playing around L.A. a lot. But they weren't really happy with the bass player, Ron. I guess they thought he wasn't keeping up with them musically. So Lars was like, 'We need a bass player. Can you recommend somebody?' And I said, 'I have the guy for you. You have to see this guy. He's incredible.' So we brought Trauma down again.

The legendary *Metal for Muthas* compilation (left) inspired Brian Slagel's historic and seminal *Metal Massacre* comp (right).

I think we brought them down again because they did really well their first gig and it was at the Troubadour and Lars came and he was just blown away. He came up to me and said, 'That guy is going to be my bass player. I'm going to get him.' And I was like all right, go ahead, good luck [laughs]. And of course, they did get him."

"Metallica happened really quick," says one of the San Francisco crew, noted photographer Bill Hale. "And I think Lars had a little playbook, a step-by-step of what he did. But not as a typical businessman. He had a sense, that rock 'n' roll sensibility or something in there that, okay, this is going to be huge. Because he knew who to contact, which people to work with, who to get on his side."

"Lars kind of had his goals set and everything," concurs Harald Oimoen, another photographer in on the ground floor in Frisco. "But I don't think he ever planned on getting this big. Nobody ever does. But I remember him saying to James one time, if they get as big as Anvil, they'll be happy. That was one of the early influences there, too. But definitely, he was always a businessman. He was always a talker. I don't think his credit in Metallica can be overstated enough. Plus the songwriting, you know? But you could kind of tell he just had this vibe about him. He had all the latest bands, knew all the latest demos, and with Ron Quintana, they would always hang out, 'Oh, I got this single that I imported that you don't have.' Like 'Blitzkrieg,' a lot of the Motörhead stuff, the first Maiden album. Yeah, he guided the ship."

Fortunately for Ulrich, Burton was becoming annoyed at the increasingly commercial direction Trauma was embracing. Metallica knew they were getting a hotshot bassist, but little did they know how much the new fat-stringer would bring to the band's musicality and songwriting, skills that wouldn't blossom until their landmark second album, *Ride the Lightning.*

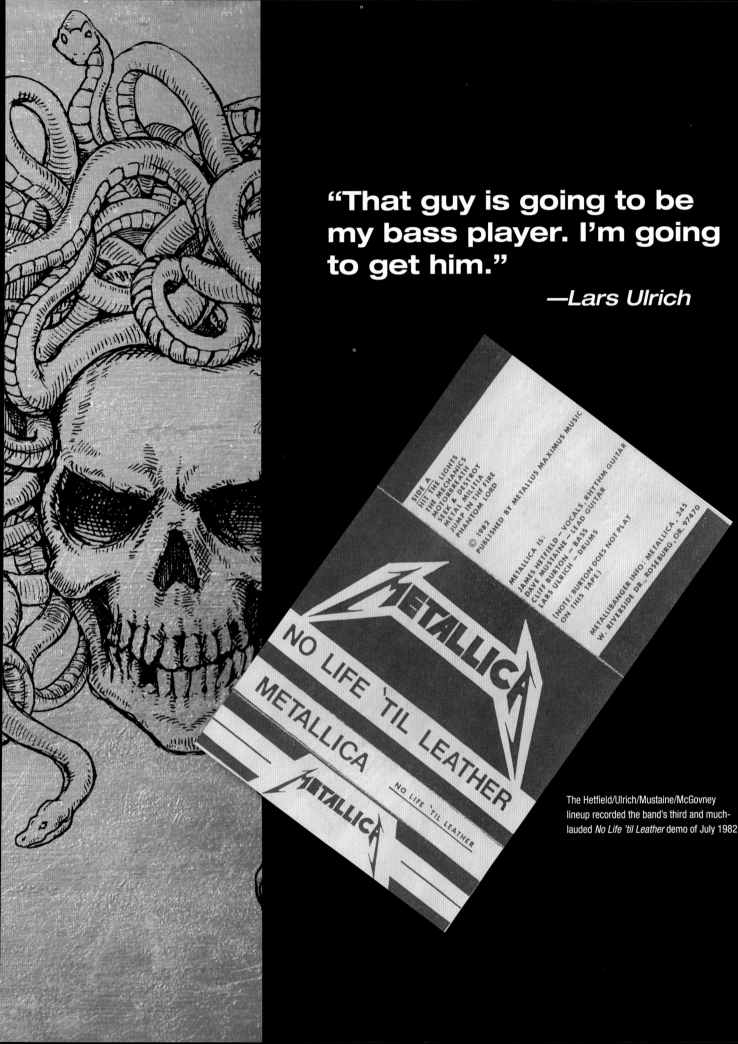

"That guy is going to be my bass player. I'm going to get him."

—Lars Ulrich

The Hetfield/Ulrich/Mustaine/McGovney lineup recorded the band's third and much-lauded *No Life 'til Leather* demo of July 1982

2.
TURN THE HELL ON
1983

"I just remember coming in there one day and he goes, 'You gotta hear this.' He had a stack of them on his counter, and he says, 'This is gonna be the new big band. I'm going to manage these guys and I'm going to get them here somehow.' I'm not sure exactly how he got them, but he had a whole stack of those cassettes."
—Jim Florentine, 2010

Armed and ready with the vicious, slicing *No Life 'til Leather* demo, it wasn't hard for Lars to get folks onto Metallica's side. One instant fan was Jon "Jonny Z" Zazula (plus his wife, Marsha), who had a record store much like Slagel's employer, Oz. It was called Rock 'n' Roll Heaven and was clear across the country in East Brunswick, New Jersey. Zazula ran the store out of a flea market on the side of the highway—all he sold was heavy metal. Rumor has it he was playing Angel Witch when he received Metallica's demo cassette, but Zazula says he was always playing Angel Witch.

The Showplace, Dover, New Jersey, April 16, 1983. When Mustaine was sent packing, Exodus guitarist Kirk Hammett helped the band pick up where they left off. This photo was taken five days after Mustaine was sacked. *Frank White Photo Agency*

"And I remember, it wasn't *No Life 'til Leather*, it was *Live at the Mab* [Author's note: Actually, *Live Metal Up Your Ass*], and it was 'The Mechanix.' I just heard that and said fuck!" recalls Zazula. "So that was unbelievable, and 'Am I Evil?' I mean, it was so great. Remember, I had every record . . . I owned every record! I listened to every record in the metal scene. It wasn't just that I sold it. You know, I *was* metal. People would come five hundred miles to talk to me about metal, Y&T, Accept, Loudness. When Randy Rhoads died, the guitarist of Ozzy, my place seemed like a church. The whole place was filled with people mourning."

And then came Metallica's first big career break: an invitation from Zazula, who was well connected in the live metal music community, thanks to a built-in audience known as the Old Bridge Metal Militia, to head east and do some shows.

"They came to my house and then they became 'Alcoholica,'" continues Zazula. "I had a little bar, with bottles of booze on it, and for somebody to drink if someone wanted a drink. And so they just took over my house, took the bottles, then left for the 18 Flea Market to meet Marsha. So my first day with them was, 'Oh my God, what did I do?' Because they were pretty crazy. Dave Mustaine got to the flea market but never made it inside. He was just standing outside with his long hair and his patches and everything, just throwing up in front of the place. And everybody knew they were from that band Metallica, so they were saying, 'What the fuck; who are these guys?' [laughs]. And Dave was always . . . you never knew what you had with Dave. He was a man of many colors."

Indeed the rest of the band was already having their doubts about Mustaine, partly because of how mean he got when drunk but also, said Hetfield at the time, due to his lack of imagination

The Stone, San Francisco, March 5, 1983. Burton, moments before jumping on stage for his first Metallica gig. © *Bill Hale*

The Stone, San Francisco, March 5, 1983. The only known photo of Burton and Mustaine alone. © *Bill Hale*

The Stone, San Francisco, March 5, 1983. © Bill Hale

The Stone, San Francisco, March 5, 1983. The only known photo of Mustaine and Hammett from back in the day. Metallica and Exodus were on the same bill. © Bill Hale

L'Amour, Brooklyn, New York, April 9,
1983. *Frank White Photo Agency*

on the guitar, calling him all speed and no feeling. "I just remember Mustaine being intoxicated all the time," says Old Bridge Militia member Jim Florentine. "I remember, we were walking through the flea market and these guys were like, 'Look, we can't take care of him. We can't deal with him anymore.' It was like noon. And I guess that was right before he was thrown out of the band."

Indeed, as the shows were winding up on the East Coast, the guys put up pretty much the last of their cash and sent Dave home on the bus, while his replacement, Exodus guitarist Kirk Hammett, helped pick up where they had left off, the next step in a whirlwind of activity being the recording of the first Metallica album.

"They sent David home because they didn't know what they were going to get," continues Zazula. "You didn't know if you were going to get a great Metallica record or just drunk, you know, fucking it up. So they brought in Kirk, which was great—that's on *Kill 'Em All*. The guy who produced the album with me [Paul Curcio] had engineered Santana's earlier albums. And he was just mixing Kirk like Carlos Santana. And the problem was, I get there at the end of the album, after being broke from finalizing the recording, and James is all depressed. And Lars has to speak to me, and he says, 'Jonny, this isn't heavy enough.' So we went in and had James redo all the rhythms, with the big, big chunky sound he's famous

John T. Comerford 111 collection/Frank White Photo Agency

The Showplace, Dover, New Jersey, April 16, 1983. *Frank White Photo Agency*

for. Because at that point, the big test with us was, beat the demo. Can we be heavier and better-sounding than the demo? Or people should just get the demo and not bother with the record? And we managed to come out flying. It was just a better-sounding demo, and it has great playing by Kirk Hammett. He went out and blazed."

Hammett fit right into the scheme of things. Soon to become prominent in the writing credits, Hammett, a San Francisco native of Filipina-Irish heritage, not only had proved himself with unsung thrash legends Exodus, but also shared Hetfield's love of Flying Vs. Reared on all the same old-school classic hard rock as the rest of the guys, he bolstered his skills by taking guitar lessons from legendary shredder Joe Satriani.

"When they did the album, they lived in people's houses in Rochester, New York," continues Zazula, but beforehand, when doing those early shows, "they stayed at Metal Joe's Funhouse in Old Bridge, New Jersey. Also, in the beginning—and it wasn't forever; it didn't last that long, but it was horrible while it did—they had the squalor of that horrible Music Building [in Queens, New York],

where Anthrax had their rehearsal space. They were in the area of the building where they threw all the things that they didn't want to take down to the garbage."

"I remember sitting in the room at the Music Building, and they had their amps kind of set up in a semicircle facing in towards Lars," recalls Anthrax's Scott Ian. "Those guys started jamming, and I was just kind of sitting there, and it was pretty much instant. It was wow, this is really intense and these guys are really, really good, and just the guitar playing right off the bat . . . they were ahead of everyone else. That's not the only reason they're one of the biggest bands in the world right now, but from that time, from '82 through '87, Metallica led the way, and the reason they led the way was that from a songwriting perspective, they were really ahead of everybody else in the game."

When all this started, Zazula didn't even have a record label, so he started Megaforce Records to sign Metallica. One wonders why Ulrich didn't sign with Brian Slagel and Metal Blade. "I think it was because I had all the shows," says Zazula. "You know, I came with

Fountain Casino, Aberdeen,
New Jersey, December 30, 1983.
Frank White Photo Agency

RT. I, NORTH BRUNSWICK, N.J. FOR INFO CA

ROYAL MAN

PRESENTS
A HEAVY METAL
SPECTACULAR
WITH

MOTÖRHEAD

WED JULY 20
TICKETS $8. IN ADVANCE
$10. AT THE DOOR

EVERY THURSDAY
AND FRIDAY JULY 15

YASGUR'S FARM

SATURDAY JULY 16

STRUTTER

COMING WEDNESDAY JULY 27
EGAFORCE RECORDS PRESENTS
VEN AND METALLICA
THE HALLOWEEN HEADBANGER BALL
ICKETS FOR MOTORHEAD ON SALE AT

RECORD SETTER
BRUNSWICK

HEAP THRILLS
BRUNSWICK

USIC STAFF
ESTFIELD

RECORD TOWNE
WOODBRIDGE
CENTER

MUSIC DEN
MONMOUTH
MALL

ROCK 'N' ROLL
HEAVEN
NEW BRUNSWICK

THINGS FROM
ENGLAND
CLIFFSIDE PARK

ALL ⊕TICKETRON OUTLETS

Rising Sun

767 YONKERS AVE.,
YONKERS, N.Y.
914-476-4662
10 MINUTES FROM GEORGE
WASHINGTON BRIDGE

WED JULY 20
ROCKBOUND
THE AIM

THURS JULY 21
MERGE
DARK WATERS

FRI JULY 22
TRILOGY
TROOPER

SAT JULY 23

Monroe

SAT JULY 29

RAVEN

& SPECIAL GUESTS

METALLICA

COMING SAT JULY 30
RAT RACE CHOIR

*Both John T. Comerford
111 collection/Frank White
Photo Agency*

All John T. Comerford 111
collection/Frank White Photo Agency

32

"I said, 'Hey, I would love to do it, but I don't have any money either.' And then they almost got a deal with some weird label in L.A., but it kinda fell through and at that point Jonny Z had got hold of the tape."

—John Kornarens

METALLICA

Merchandise
"KILL 'EM ALL" T-SHIRT
Full-color, 2-sided black t-shirt with
cover art work on front,
"Bang that Head . . ." on back.
$10.00 S,M,L

M.U.Y.A. T-SHIRT
Black with white logo and *M.U.Y.A.*
$8.00 S,M,L

ENAMEL BADGE
Red logo on gold pin
$3.00

BUTTON
Red logo on black background
$1.00

SEW-ON PATCH
$5.00

Send check or money order payable to: Metallica
Metal Militia, 345 W. Riverside Dr., Roseburg,
OR 97470 U.S.A. (American Currency Only)
Please add $1.50 per item for shipping,
$2.00 overseas. Please allow 6-8 weeks for
delivery. Guaranteed Airmail Overseas
You can purchase Metallica's debut
album, "Kill 'Em All" on Megaforce
records at finer record stores .
nationwide.

Watch For New Single "Jump In The Fire" W Live "Seek And Destroy" Available Nov. 15

1983 merch letter.
Frank White collection

Venom shows, Twisted Sister shows, Vandenberg shows, all kinds of fans where they could play in front of, lots of people—and on the East Coast. So they were testing me all the way through, and I kept delivering. Remember, by the time we finished touring Metallica, under the Crazed Management umbrella, they were a big band already—they could probably do three thousand themselves. In some markets, not in all markets."

Slagel, however, intimates that it came down to not having the cash to make it happen. "It was John Kornarens that had first got the demo tape from Lars. John had come to the record store—this is when I was still working at the record store—and he said, 'Hey, I want to play something.' And I said yeah, whatever. And he put the tape in and said, 'You have to guess who this is.' And he puts the tape in and it's really good and I'm going, 'Wow, who is this?' And he goes, 'This is Metallica.' 'This is Metallica?!' This is the first *No Life 'til Leather* demo and it was amazing. So they had come to me and said, 'Hey, we want to put a record out, but we don't have any money'. . . . And I said, 'Hey, I would love to do it, but I don't have any money either.' Because they needed eight thousand dollars to record the record. And nobody had that kind of money. . . . And then they almost got a deal with some weird label in L.A., but it kinda fell through and at that point Jonny Z had got hold of the tape and said, 'Hey, I'll do it.'"

Kill 'Em All, issued July 25, 1983, in an initial pressing of fifteen thousand, would essentially redefine what it meant to be heavy metal. It wasn't that the record was a complete reinvention of anything. Certainly the likes of

The original concept for the LP that became *Kill 'Em All*.

www.WycoVintage.com

Raven and Anvil were, in spots, this heavy, this speedy, this technical. What placed *Kill 'Em All* a hammer blow above was the uneasy feeling that it was relentless, faces pressed forward, so many superlative riffs, so little time, and all of them played aggressively, Hetfield reinforcing the violence with a vocal that, like the music, was just a little more purely metal than anything previous.

The album title and accompanying cover art reinforced the sonic mayhem. Originally, the plan was to call it *Metal Up Your Ass*, the wrapper to feature a hand holding a knife emerging from a toilet. Zazula pleaded with the guys to reconsider, saying no distributor would stock it, and the classier and yet equally painful *Kill 'Em All* suggested by Burton was agreed upon, the attendant graphic showing a puddle of blood, a hammer and a hand dropping it, job done.

Job done, indeed. The album opens with yet another recording of "Hit the Lights," this one introducing listeners to the album's sharp, powerful, no-nonsense production, all the better to highlight Hetfield's quick picking hand and the band's tightness. Representing the chugging, less accelerated face and pace of Metallica is second track "The Four Horsemen," along with "Jump in the Fire," "Seek & Destroy," and "No Remorse," each crammed with money riffs that form a

bridge from Sabbath to Pantera. "Seek & Destroy," says Hetfield, was based on Diamond Head non-LPer "Dead Reckoning," adding that he wrote that riff while sitting in his truck outside of the sticker factory where he worked. "The Four Horsemen" was a reworking of the Mustaine-penned "The Mechanix" (Mustaine is credited on four *Kill 'Em All* tracks). The track reemerged as "Mechanix" on Mustaine's first record after his Metallica ousting, Megadeth's *Killing Is My Business . . . and Business Is Good!*, which in turn set up Mustaine for a lifetime of resentfully shadowing his former band, a situation with which he has only recently come to terms.

As for the rest of *Kill 'Em All*, much of it was shockingly fast, especially "Whiplash," "Phantom Lord," and "Metal Militia," an anthem for a new, angrier breed of metalhead. This is where Metallica was forging new pathways, establishing themselves on the scene as the heaviest band around, even if Slayer and Venom might have had something to say about that.

It seems apt that Metallica's first album opens with "Hit the Lights," the first tune James Hetfield and Lars Ulrich ever wrote together. It's also a song in which the young Het sings about the actual act of playing and performing heavy metal. Somewhat standard-issue NWOBHM-style boogie-metal workout, only jacked up to teeth-rattling, speed-freak tempos, it's a pretty fine introductory jam.

You can take it further: As "Lights" represents the embryonic Metallica (in particular given the fact that there are also earlier recorded versions, with various players filling the lead guitar and bass slots, on the *Metal Massacre* compilation and assorted demos), so does *Kill 'Em All* signify the birth of the thrash movement. While discriminating heshers endlessly debate whether or not it truly is The First Thrash Metal Album Ever, in the end it doesn't much matter: *Kill 'Em All* without question gave rise to innumerable thrash bands and fans.

In retrospect it's not hard to see why. There's the awesome speed, the revolutionary (for the time) blending of Brit-metal bombast—think Priest, Maiden, and especially Diamond Head—with the street-level aggression of hardcore punk, and the fierce technical edge of the music, best exemplified by Hetfield's aggressively downpicked, heavily palm-muted rhythm-guitar attack.

Then again, these elements were also evident, in differing combinations, in the sounds of other nascent thrashers dotting the landscape at the time, from Slayer to Exodus to Anthrax. Where *Kill 'Em All* stood apart from the pack was in its embrace of a more blue-collar (for lack of a better term) ethos, as well as a sense of rock tradition. To put it simply, you felt like you knew where these guys were coming from. Kirk Hammett burned the fretboard, but also opted more for bluesy pentatonic patterns and Schenker-ish melody lines than whammy-bar tricks and exotic scalar runs. Hetfield's gruff, shout/speak delivery, meanwhile, was gut-level direct.

KILL 'EM ALL

by Richard Bienstock

Say what you will about the allure of Slayer or Exodus, but Tom Araya or Paul Baloff hardly represented the everyman. Hetfield, however, sounded *just like you*. Only tougher—and way more metal.

Which is not to say that Metallica didn't fall victim to some of the more embarrassing metal clichés of the day here. There's the goofily fantastical imagery—four horsemen riding leather steeds, a phantom lord with sword in hand—that seemed to ensnare almost every early-'80s metal band not named Motörhead. There are also, in addition to "Lights," two more songs ("Metal Militia" and "Whiplash") about heavy metal itself. But mostly there is just classic music, like the epic—lyrics be damned—"The Four Horsemen" (one of four tunes on the album co-penned by Dave Mustaine, it would appear, under its earlier title "Mechanix," on Megadeth's '85 debut), the stop-start power-groover "Motorbreath," and the circular and riffy "Jump in the Fire."

But if there's a moment on *Kill 'Em All* that best illustrates Metallica's early prowess and hints at their future potential, it's the penultimate track, "Seek & Destroy." It's certainly not the fastest cut on the album (actually, it's the slowest), or even the best (credit here goes perhaps to the rampaging "Whiplash") or most extreme (see Cliff Burton's fuzz-bass freakout, "[Anesthesia]–Pulling Teeth"), but it is arguably the most well composed, boasting bluesy, uncluttered riffs, a hooky, shout-along chorus refrain, and an economical (save for a midsong double-time rave-up) arrangement. It's hardly groundbreaking, but compared to their peers at the time, Metallica's respect for and adherence to rock tradition here seems almost radical. On *Kill 'Em All* Metallica set about recombining their influences in order to remap rock 'n' roll's borders—and drag us all into a louder, faster world.

The Music for Nations 12-inch
EP—with crowd noise added.

The odd track out was "(Anesthesia)–Pulling Teeth," a bass solo from Burton, who, like Hetfield and Mustaine, had experienced personal pain early in life, in his case through the death of a brother. It is said that he switched from piano and classical music lessons to heavy metal and electric bass around the time of this family tragedy and vowed to be the best bassist in the world, in tribute to his brother. His solid traditional musical upbringing, however, along with his appreciation of jazz, prog, and southern rock, helped make him an important contributor to the assembly of the early Metallica canon. It was Burton's dexterity on "(Anesthesia)–Pulling Teeth" as performed with Trauma that convinced Hetfield and Ulrich to ditch the underachieving McGovney for Burton.

"The difference between *Kill 'Em All* and *Ride the Lightning* and *Master of Puppets*," Ulrich told me, "is sort of the old cliché about how you have your whole life to write your first record and then you have, what, three months to write your second record. It's a different process when you walk into a studio with a pile of songs that you have been playing for years, that you've played in front of an audience dozens and dozens of times. Some of the songs on *Kill 'Em All*, we'd been playing for two years, you know what I mean? They sit differently in your body than something you wrote the day before [laughs]. So it becomes more like executing something; it becomes executing more than creating. So *Kill 'Em All*, when I hear stuff from that album, I hear youth and I hear ignorance. Sometimes the words ignorance and innocence run dangerously close to each other. But I hear youthful innocence."

"Sometimes we joke that it doesn't quite sound like James' balls have dropped yet," laughs Ulrich. "We were very young back then, and there's a pure type of energy in that. . . . When I think of that record, you know, we had never made a record before. There were

Frank White collection

"Mechanix" would reemerge on Mustaine's first record after his Metallica ousting, Megadeth's *Killing Is My Business . . . and Business Is Good!*, which set him up for a lifetime of resentfully shadowing his former band. *Author collection*

"Back then it was a lot rarer to actually put a f***ing record out. So we were pretty f***ing pumped about that."

—Lars Ulrich

some money issues and there were some experiences where me and James stayed behind to mix the record with this guy, and we went down to the studio to give our two cents on the mixing and stuff and they wouldn't let us in. So the mixing was done . . . I have this vision and picture of, like, standing outside the studio door ringing the doorbell for half an hour, and we knew they were in there. It was kind of like fucked up. When it's your first record, I mean, you're just so proud and you're so psyched. I mean, now it's almost commonplace with all the independent labels and everything to put records out. That thing is not special now, but back then it was a lot rarer to actually put a fucking record out. So we were pretty fucking pumped about that."

Vagabonds of the Western world that they were, Metallica gigged in the East, recorded the album, and then stayed on the East Coast to begin touring the new album, first up and down the seaboard, then into middle America, down to Texas, and finally back across to California in September 1983, eventually hitting home turf, The Stone in San Francisco, on November 7. They wouldn't stay long in their newly adopted home, hitting the road again almost immediately. Early dates were in support of proto-thrashers Raven (a couple steps ahead of Metallica and a crucial influence) on a two-month jaunt called Kill 'Em All for One, Raven supporting their *All for One* album, a classic that found that band oddly abdicating thrash for slower, more grinding and powerful terrain, leaving the door open for Metallica to pounce.

The *Kill 'Em All* campaign was finally crowned by the band's first trip to Europe, in February 1984, on the Seven Dates of Hell tour, in support of yet another crucial thrash inventor, Venom, with Twisted Sister also supporting. February 11 saw the band play to their biggest crowd yet, seven thousand, as part of Holland's Aardshock Festival. Jonny Zazula had by this point set up an agreement with U.K.'s Music for Nations label (regrets soon to follow), who thought it wise to issue some product to commemorate the tour. The result was the *Jump in the Fire* 12-inch with a sleeve featuring, for no apparent reason, a ghoulish monster, along with music comprising "live" songs—"Seek & Destroy," "Phantom Lord," and the toe-tapping title track—recorded in the studio with crowd noise added.

Having looked outside themselves by sharing stages with two of the best of the new extreme metal bands—Raven and Venom—as well as having looked within at their very substantial capabilities, Metallica were ready to craft the thrash masterpiece they knew they had in them.

3.
LIGHTNING TO THE NATIONS
1984—1985

"If you haven't heard of Metallica, you must've been too busy getting a Duran haircut. Any metal lover knows these boys are gonna be the next mega-metallers. No, they don't wear eye shadow, but they sure as hell crank out tunes."
—Marilyn Bajus, *Metallion*, 1984

Despite its palpable magic, *Kill 'Em All* wasn't exactly a work of musical genius. But Metallica would make more than good on the record's promise given a second chance. Writing sessions for what would become *Ride the Lightning* took place in late 1983 with recording the following spring in Copenhagen, of all expensive places, production courtesy of Sweet Silence Studios owner and engineer Flemming Rasmussen, who prior to Metallica had produced only Rainbow, albeit twice. The band worried that too much of the record featured songs created in the studio, but their confidence had built, and they had much more control of everything, including the electric chair cover art concept, their idea from the start. (An interesting side note, Zazula says the band almost chose Par Studios in Florida on the strength of the walloping sound achieved on Savatage's debut album, *Sirens*.)

A buzz band becomes an above-ground success. *Fin Costello/Redferns/Getty Images*

"They were in the studio for a very long time," recalls Zazula, asked about his first impressions upon hearing *Ride*, "and they now took a break in England, because the album was supposed to be done. We had gone through our entire budget for recording the album. And I came to England to hear the album, and all it was was some bass and drums. The whole album had yet to be recorded. So when I *did* hear the album and I heard the songs, it was like the second coming. You know, you just knew. You just knew, just like the third album. They just kept doing it! They kept coming up with these fucking songs, man. And that's the great story of Metallica. They had songs. And boy, did they have songs."

However, there were studio problems, as Ulrich explained to *Metal Forces'* Bernard Doe, credited with

Megaforce owner Jonny Z at his home office in Old Bridge, New Jersey, 1986. *Frank White photo*

42

writing the first major feature on the band. "The initial sound problems you spoke about was [sic] really due to all our gear getting ripped off just three weeks before we got to Copenhagen," Ulrich said. "For instance, James had this one-in-a-million Marshall head that he lost, and he had problems getting the rhythm sound he was looking for and the sound that Metallica are known for. We probably went through every Marshall in Denmark, including all of Mercyful Fate's gear, before finding one that was right."

Ride the Lightning was a vaulted leap over *Kill 'Em All* in every department. Opener "Fight Fire with Fire," after being birthed by a renaissance music diddle, explodes into a classic of superhuman speed, an example of what

John T. Comerford 111 collection/Frank White Photo Agency

A Midsummer Night's Scream, Roseland Ballroom, New York City, August 3, 1984. *Both © Bob Leafe*

metal could achieve. The title track features rhythmic complexity similar to the opening salvo, while the band demonstrates superstar-savvy pacing and sequencing by following up with the triumphant elephantine classic "For Whom the Bell Tolls," the side closing with doom-drenched power ballad "Fade to Black."

Side two features a superfast *Kill 'Em All* redux called "Trapped Under Ice," followed by the shockingly catchy mid-pacer "Escape," Metallica plotting their first steps toward "Enter Sandman." Huge Metallica now-classic "Creeping Death" is brisk but not thrash of pace, its construction benefiting from Rasmussen's billowy, warm production dominated by stone-carved rhythm guitars. *Ride* closes with the sophisticated nine-minute instrumental "The Call of Ktulu," the band referencing H. P. Lovecraft with this classical-minded metal sledge.

"The difference with *Ride the Lightning*, compared with *Kill 'Em All*, is that it's not like just one complete track like *Kill 'Em All* was," Ulrich told Doe at the time. "And the way it's different is because not all the tracks are played at 'Metal Militia' speed. You see, the one thing we realized about making *Kill 'Em All* and *Ride the Lightning* was that you don't have to depend on speed to be powerful and heavy. I think songs like 'For Whom the Bell Tolls' and 'Ride the Lightning' reflect that sort of attitude. I think generally most people have received it favorably and certainly a lot better than I think anyone in the band thought it would. OK, there's always the odd letter or comment like, 'If you don't play ten "Metal Militias" on every album, then it's not Metallica and it's not good,' but we're doing what we're doing the way we feel at a certain time. The band has matured and we're still learning. If people think we're wimping out, then fuck 'em; we don't need that kinda shit."

"I honestly believe that the kids who are into the Priest, Maiden, KISS, Sister thing will take onto what we're doing," Ulrich continued, perceptively commenting on the condition the band was exerting upon metal fans. "I'm not saying it's something that's going to happen overnight, but it could gradually start developing and Metallica could be the frontrunners of a new branch of heavy metal. Also, we haven't had to change to do it."

"Ultimate thrash, destruction and total blur sums it up," wrote *Grinder*'s Kevin Fisher, reviewing the album. "Metallica's second LP *Ride the Lightning* delivers a lot of speed and power, like the first LP does. 'Fight Fire with Fire' is the heaviest song on the album, gaining speeds of 100 mph; it rips your house apart and is a total blur. The second song, 'Ride the Lightning,' is another cut that rips your face from your head and throws you against the wall. 'Trapped Under Ice' is a pretty killer song; the only problem with it is that it is exactly like Exodus' 'Impaler' with a couple riffs from 'Hell's Breath.' 'Creeping Death' has some riffs from Exodus' 'Die by His Hand.' Other standouts are 'For Whom the Bell Tolls' and 'Fade to Black,' which shows the more melodic and musical part of Metallica. The last song on the album, 'The Call of Ktulu,' originally called 'When Hell Freezes Over,' delivers nine minutes of straightforward power with a little melodic touch. So, for all you metal maniacs who don't have this album, buy it or die!"

"Don't let the first track fool ya," seconded *Metallion*'s Marilyn Bajus, before going on to offer a cheeky side comment on Iron Maiden's *Powerslave* released the same year: "'Fight Fire with Fire' starts off soft and pretty, but quickly engulfs your brain 'til you're helplessly hooked and begging for more. Never fear, *Ride the Lightning* truly satisfies. Metallica's got the formula for some of

L'Amour, Brooklyn, New York, January 25, 1985.
Frank White Photo Agency

For more than twenty years, Metallica has been one of the top-selling acts in the world. But there was a time when there was nothing more badass than sporting their back patch on your denim vest. It pretty much disqualified you from polite society, and their 1984 sophomore outing, *Ride the Lightning*, is a big reason why. The album heralded something new. It had sophistication and brutality in equal measure, and it served notice that Metallica could not be written off.

The album kicks off deceptively with elegant, chiming major-key acoustic guitars. Forty-one seconds later we're thrown in at the deep end with the panicked and persistent beatdown of "Fight Fire with Fire." It has everything you needed to know about speed metal, circa 1984, from the stuttering palm-muted guitar to the hail of double-bass drums to the lyrics about nuclear war.

The opener gives way to the anti–death penalty title track. It starts with straight, midtempo riffing, which, thanks to James Hetfield's downpicking, sounded absolutely revolutionary at the time. The song's not prog, but it has enough twists and melodic sophistication to permanently remove Metallica from Venom territory. The song is also distinguished by a lengthy instrumental middle section, in which Kirk Hammett stretches out with an incredibly lyrical Uli Roth–channeling lead that never stops telling a story.

"For Whom the Bell Tolls" is a bona fide anthem that took Metallica further into territory that most of their speed metal brethren would never see. After giving listeners a solid chromatic pummeling for the first minute or so, it shifts into something more atmospheric, emotional, and unmistakably classic, something that makes it clear why a Metallica set without this song is unthinkable.

RIDE THE LIGHTNING

RIDE THE LIGHTNING

by Daniel Bukszpan

The last song on side one, "Fade to Black," was controversial. The suicide anthem was not only the group's most ambitious song to date, but also a clear indication that Metallica had a muse to follow, even if it meant occasionally courting ridicule or risking appearing soft. It didn't work out that way, however, and with "Fade," Metallica had their own "Stairway to Heaven" and it let them start sneaking into the mainstream.

Side two is less risky and therefore less of a revelation than side one. There's nothing bad on it, but after the heights scaled on side one, "Trapped Under Ice" and "Escape" seem forgettable and average. But momentum is recovered, big time, with "Creeping Death." Though the song sounds pretty dated today—there's faster and heavier stuff out there for sure—goddamn, it gets you worked up and makes you want to run outside and put a sledgehammer through the windshield of the nearest parked car.

The song gives way to the instrumental "The Call of Ktulu," which despite some great riffs has no real reason to stretch on to almost nine minutes. Then as now, Metallica had yet to receive the memo stating that you only need to repeat a riff four times instead of sixteen, thank you very much. But by the time the song starts to drag, you're too fully invested in the album to complain, much less turn it off.

Ride the Lightning is a fast, pummeling, brutally heavy album that could scare the living shit out of your parents, your classmates, and your girlfriend. It was one of the most antisocial statements you could put on a turntable. But there's more to it than that. It's also the rare album of the speed metal era that could be said to have soul, depth, and beauty, and to provide something comforting during the sustained beating.

Hetfield and Pantera's Dimebag Darrell jam in the latter's bedroom at his mother's home in Arlington, Texas, September 1985. *Frank White photo*

Hardcore Happenings
PRESENTS
METALLICA
WITH SPECIAL GUESTS
OVER KILL & *Anti*
AT THE
STATE THEATER
131 PIKE ST., PORT JERVIS, N.Y.
FOR INFO CALL 914-856-8444
TICKETS $8.00 ADVANCE $10.00 AT DOOR

Jan. 4, 1984/page 15 (5-A)

John T. Comerford 111 collection/ Frank White Photo Agency

48

the fastest and heaviest music, without crossing over to noise. The menacingly ominous 'For Whom the Bell Tolls' is a slower sample but keeps the Metallica sharp edge. The attack continues with 'Trapped Under Ice.' This one includes some of the most frantic drumming and steamiest leads this side of Venom on speed. One of the best cuts is 'Fade to Black.' Its beginning soothes your ears with stirring acoustic guitar work from Kirk Hammett, then it changes and changes again, spanning many moods and swift tempo changes that keep you guessing. You'd expect such a heavy band not to have worthwhile lyrics. Look again. They may be a bit too pessimistic, but that seems to be the latest trend in '80s metal. 'Creeping Death' is one example—that's a song you're not going to sit through! But what's with the Egyptian kick everyone seems to be on lately?"

Jonny Zazula was already looking ahead, trying to figure out the delicate dance of maneuvering the band into the hands of a major label.

"I have to tell you something," Zazula begins. "First of all, Marsha and I didn't know anything about the business. We performed a miracle. We took every penny we owned, we didn't pay our mortgage, we didn't pay to have the records in the shop, we were up to our ears, we believed we had the next Led Zeppelin and the next God knows what. . . . Now, in my later years, I have a tremendous sense of what it is to be a manager, and to be a record company geek. I didn't know then where I was at, but I do know that I didn't know much. I thought I did [laughs]. And by the way, that scared people, because remember, Metallica didn't want to be the one thing that I made famous. They didn't know that I would have success with Anthrax and Ministry and Testament, and somewhat of a success with Kings X and Ace Frehley. We sold four hundred thousand of all that stuff. So if they would've known, things would've been a little bit different. But they were worried."

Author collection

Poperinge, Belgium, 1984. *Author collection*

STUFF 'EM ALL!
Tell your wimp friends to listen to some **real** metal...VENOM!

venom

WELCOME TO HELL
BRC 1907

At War with Satan

BLACK METAL
BRC 1908

PolyGram

BANZAI RECORDS
POLYGRAM DISTRIBUTION INC.

Metallion opined "Trapped Under the Ice" sounded like "Venom on speed." *Author collection*

> "I think as an A&R person with really good instincts, I think I know when somebody really is a star and has that kind of quality, and I just found that they were the most charismatic band that I had ever seen."
>
> —*Michael Alago*

"It was all part of one big plan," Zazula sighs. "As I said, on one hand, I wanted to build this Megaforce label, but on the other hand, I truly believed that the bands should go to the next level. They have to get signed to majors. And I thought it would be the end of Megaforce, actually, but it just kept going. You know, everything just kept going. I have to tell you, it was like being on a luge. It was just one big fast ride. It was all happening so fast back then. All I had to do was touch something and everybody wanted it."

"There were some indie labels, but it was ridiculous," Zazula continues, addressing the offers that started to come in for Metallica. "They didn't want to give that much money, and those that wanted to give money would come to me and say, 'The introduction from "For Whom the Bell Tolls" has to be cut back from a minute,' and I said, 'I don't think these guys are going to do that. [laughs] These guys won't do that.' And then I had the fellow who is A&R for Sony; he didn't get it at all. And basically, we were so excited with the pitch, that we left our one and

only cassette player with the tape. And nobody got it. I played the Anthrax for somebody, who was the head of Arista at the time, and he ducked under his desk. He couldn't take the sheer volume of the beginning of the Anthrax album. It scared him. And I won't give names, but he knows who he is. And he's still in business today."

A deal was coming though, and quickly, but before that, Zazula had printed up seventy-five thousand copies of *Ride the Lightning* on Megaforce, with Music for Nations pulling a fast one by printing their own run and then exporting them to the States, which Zazula says was definitely against their deal.

Metallica would wind up on Elektra Records, thanks to the enthusiasm of a young A&R hotshot named Michael Alago. "I think as an A&R person with really good instincts, I think I know when somebody really is a star and has that kind of quality," Alago says. "And I just found that they were the most charismatic band that I had ever seen. Everything else fucking pales into comparison, when you see James on stage. James is a fucking ringleader.

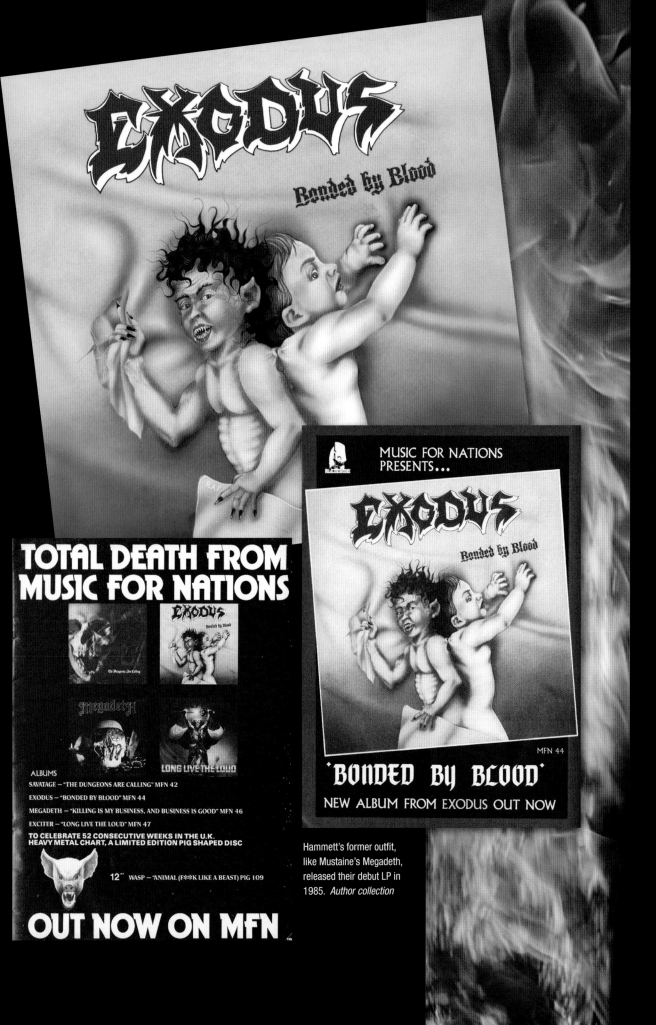

EXODUS
Bonded by Blood

MUSIC FOR NATIONS PRESENTS...

EXODUS
Bonded by Blood

MFN 44

'BONDED BY BLOOD'

NEW ALBUM FROM EXODUS OUT NOW

Hammett's former outfit,
like Mustaine's Megadeth,
released their debut LP in
1985. *Author collection*

The late-July release of *Ride the Lightning* was followed by the *Creeping Death* EP, which found Metallica paying homage to Diamond Head. *Author collection*

He knew how to whip the crowd into a frenzy each and every night. I started doing A&R in March of 1983 and no other A&R person was interested in them at a major label. Jonny Z was still managing them with Marsha. . . . I'd heard *Kill 'Em All* at some point and I'm just freaking out because I've never heard anything like that before. I had to figure out, 'Oh Jesus, fucking Jonny will kill me if I try to sign them to Elektra.' So I wound up, I think, going to The Stone in San Francisco, and I saw the guys there and they were fabulous; we talked a little bit. And I said, 'Well, when you come to New York please tell me, because I want to invite the chairman of our company, the head of promotion, and all these people, to the gig. So fast-forward, I don't talk to Lars for six or seven months, I'm doing these demos with Raven, they tell me they're coming August of '84 to the Roseland with Raven

and Anthrax. Okay, perfect timing. So I go see them and I lose my mind. Right after the show was over I made a beeline backstage, practically bolted the door shut. And I said, 'You know what? I'm crazy about y'all, I want you in my life, it's the most extraordinary thing I've ever heard.' And I think they liked me as much as I liked them. Because I was young and crazy and loved the music. And so after Roseland, the next day, they came up to my office. I got beer and Chinese food and they never left."

"Michael had had an interest in the band and was crazy about James," confirms Zazula. "And we were just proceeding and proceeding, and then I guess it was, I don't know how it transpired away from me, but I think what happened was, as we were developing the deal, we were losing the band. So there was no sense in going forward. What cinched all the deals was the Midsummer's

Night Scream that we held at the Roseland Ballroom. We did the first shows at the Roseland Ballroom that were metal. . . . And that night, everybody came to see what the hell was going on. We were under a real microscope. And that night I saw the head of Elektra . . . I figured, well that's where that's definitely going. And I really paid it no mind, because you have to realize, when you are working with people, if they don't want to work with you, what? Are they going to make you crazy? It's not worth it. It's just . . . you have a life to live. And it was getting a little crazy at that point."

"We all knew what was going down, but we were tightlipped," continues Zazula. "[The band] didn't want to come out and tell me, and I didn't want to ask any questions, but I knew, and we just let it take shape, rather than having conversations about it. You know, I never had a conversation, 'I broke you guys, I made you guys, blah, blah, blah, I gave you your first album.' I never

had that conversation with them. It was like, if you feel after all this, you have to go, then by all means, let's work out something legally. Which I don't discuss."

With metal taking off, Alago knew Metallica was special and didn't worry about the next signing so much. "Yes, for me, I didn't care because I felt I had the best band," he says. "A lot of people got away with murder after I signed Metallica. Everybody was getting signed. Everybody wanted something that sounded like that. I mean, there are a lot of great bands out there, but people played follow the leader, when they saw that Elektra was taking that chance. But a lot of great bands came out of that whole period . . . there are so many records that I ended up loving and thinking, this has nothing. . . . I mean, we all loved and grew up with Iron Maiden and Judas Priest and Black Sabbath and Deep Purple and Ozzy. But all this new stuff, in a weird way, I don't want to say it had nothing to do with that. . . . . But Metallica was

Author collection

www.WycoVintage.com

54

www.WycoVintage.com

just something so fucking new and fresh and different and loud. It was a little bit of punk, a little bit of thrash, a little bit of old school. If you are any good at all, you use all those references, like Metallica did, and you call that your own thing."

"Metallica were really in a class of their own," agrees John Strednansky. "But some people were still shocked that they got the major deal. I remember that. There was discussion like, 'Oh my God, we don't believe it.' There was some disbelief, because at the time majors still had the image of just catering to the real commercial stuff. A couple of years prior, with Riot's *Fire Down Under* . . . it was what, '81? Capitol said flat-out, no, we're not going to sign this, it's not gonna sell, it's too heavy. And Elektra picked it up. That kind of opened some doors for Metallica."

The late-July release of *Ride the Lightning* was followed by the *Creeping Death* EP, which found Metallica paying homage to their biggest influence, Diamond Head, through the inclusion of that band's "Am I Evil?," which has proven to be a Metallica live favorite over the years. Also on tap was the catchy NWOBHM nugget "Blitzkrieg," originally by Blitzkrieg. This all helped make Metallica a definite buzz band, and *Ride the Lightning* first an underground success and, by November of '87, an above-ground success. On that date the album would go gold, tugged there by the success of its world-beating follow-up *Master of Puppets*.

Touring for the record found the band hitting Europe first, supporting Tank, yet another closely related "extreme" metal band, sort of the thinking man's Motörhead. The Bang That Head That Doesn't Bang tour lasted about a month, beginning in mid-November, after which Metallica returned to the States for a January–March 1985 leg coheadlining with W.A.S.P., with Armored Saint as support. The band's biggest U.S. show yet came on August 31 as part of one of Bill Graham's Day on the Green packages, the confused state of metal demonstrated by a lineup that included Scorpions, Ratt, Yngwie Malmsteen, and San Francisco's first hard rock heroes, Y&T.

But the highlight of the year was the band's first Monsters of Rock at Donington, England, on August 17, playing to a crowd of seventy thousand, many of them hurling projectiles at this band they clearly didn't understand. Metallica was by far the heaviest on a bill that also included progsters Magnum and Marillion, hair bands Bon Jovi and Ratt, and headliners ZZ Top. A passing of the guard was angrily suggested by Hetfield, who famously exhorted from the stage, "If you came here to see spandex and fuckin' eye makeup and all that shit . . . and the words, 'Ooh baby' in every fuckin' song, this ain't the fuckin' band. We came here to bash some fuckin' heads for fifty minutes. Are you fuckin' with us?"

4.
THIS MEANS WAR
1986–1987

"I thought it might be a little too crazy for most people. I'm glad I was wrong."
—Cliff Burton on the success of *Master of Puppets*, *Hit Parader*, 1986

With everything becoming manic around the band, writing and demo sessions for a third Metallica record occurred in fits and starts between July 1985 and the end of the year, marbled with sporadic live commitments.

All sorts of heavy metal was selling well by this point, the axis having shifted from the United Kingdom to California, with most of the old guard from the '70s—Judas Priest, Ozzy Osbourne, Scorpions, Deep Purple, KISS—enjoying a second wind as well. Still, there wasn't much of the stronger stuff around, other than the likes of Slayer, Anthrax, and Metal Church, to test the market. Essentially, all eyes were on Metallica, who seemed to be shoving their way into the mainstream on pure talent alone, having ridden *Ride the Lightning* to No. 100 on the *Billboard* charts.

Shoving their way into the mainstream, 1986. *Krasner/Trebitz /Redferns/Getty Images*

Meadowlands Arena, East Rutherford,
New Jersey, April 21, 1986. © *Bob Leafe*

Decades down the road, Hetfield still recalls with disdain the metal-lite that was the domain of his home state, telling Greg Pratt that his present-day onstage personality was forged from "twenty-seven years of playing live and growing up in Los Angeles, disliking the music scene. I think a lot of the persona did develop out of where we came from. The speed, the intensity, the loudness, we wanted the attention. Growing up in Los Angeles playing with all the glam bands when the scene was all about looks, hair, whatever . . . we were certainly not about that; we wanted music, we had to play louder, faster, for people to notice us. And you know, along with your normal mannerisms that's part of what you develop, and it's your sword up there, it's your shield, it's your everything, you're able to hide behind it, you're able to go further than I would just sitting here talking to you. I think it's taking your body, your voice, your soul, your being to a higher elevation. When you get on stage, there's something. I certainly wouldn't do the things I do up there in front of my family at Thanksgiving [laughs]—I wouldn't. The music and the people take me somewhere. It's like the Olympics for us [laughs]. You go farther."

Sessions for what would become *Master of Puppets* were to be produced and mixed once again by Flemming Rasmussen at Sweet Silence. However, the band ran over time and Rasmussen couldn't stick around to mix, so the band and their top-flight management (at this point Cliff Burnstein, Peter Mensch, and Q Prime) hired on Michael Wagener, beloved for his work with Raven and Accept. Ulrich would express his appreciation for Wagener's ability to stand by his convictions yet bend if the band had a good idea. That team, with Metallica

Tarrant County Coliseum, Fort Worth, Texas, May 10, 1986. *Stuart Taylor photo/Frank White Photo Agency*

Cain's Ballroom, Tulsa, Oklahoma,
May 23, 1986. *All © Rich Galbraith*

sharing production credit, constructed a wholly different production palette than that heard on *Ride the Lightning*, yet one every bit as powerful, carnal, and wondrously excessive.

Master of Puppets offers, for better or worse, an almost track-for-track matchup with the dramatic and painterly peaks and valleys that was *Ride the Lightning*. Bookends to the record, "Battery" and "Damage, Inc." provide the speed and rhythmic tightness and dexterity that Metallica (and to some extent Anthrax) made famous. "Disposable Heroes" and the epic title track bridge "Creeping Death" to the excesses of Metallica's next record, . . . *And Justice For All*, each of those tracks nonetheless world-beating examples of the smart possibilities of thrash put into the hands of a band with tear-away talent.

Cliff Burton's contribution is heard on instrumental "Orion," the song's slightly classical sensibility adding richness, Metallica managing to write an interesting no-vocals proposition for the second record in a row. Hanging with *Sounds*' Steffan Chirazzi and monitoring the mix, Cliff indicated, "That's why I'm down, man. Because there's some very complicated bass at the beginning of 'Orion,' which only I can supervise." Added Ulrich, "That is undoubtedly our biggest strength at the moment; no one can simply write off Metallica as being thrash. The first album was, we know that, but this album is a totally different proposition. ['Orion' is] about nine minutes long, but those who've heard

Above: Asking the label execs to buzz them in. Rockefeller Center, New York City, December 2, 1986. *Frank White photo*

Left and right: Capitol Theatre, Passaic, New Jersey, November 29, 1986. *Both © Bob Leafe*

it say it sounds half that time, because it's not purely shitty indulgence."

"Welcome Home (Sanitarium)" is more deceptively a ballad than "Fade to Black" was, most of it quite briskly thrashing, Hetfield having written it partly as an homage to *One Flew Over the Cuckoo's Nest*, partly reflective of his homesickness as the days dragged on in Copenhagen. "I know that on this album the fast ones are some of the fastest we've ever written!" Hetfield noted at the time. "We never try to forget what Metallica formed for, no way. It's just that maturity in style breeds better material all 'round. Metallica now is variety with spice. As you could hear, on a lot of numbers, there are little things that demand a lot of attention. Those vocals have to be just right to create that hollow effect on 'Welcome Home (Sanitarium),' and Lars is real fussy about his

Both author collection

Monsters of Rock, Castle Donington, England, August 22, 1987. *Mike Cameron/Redferns/Getty Images*

When Metallica's third album, *Master of Puppets*, was released in 1986, some grumbled that the band had sold out. The production, performances, and songwriting are more polished than on *Ride the Lightning*, and, thus, the band's fortunes improved considerably. Still, some facts are in order.

First, the record received no airplay. None. In fact, it received no mainstream promotion of any kind. It sold a half-million copies by word of mouth and by the band busting their asses on the road. In fact, the music industry embraced Metallica because the sheer number of units the band shifted without them meant they had to. The cream had simply risen to the top.

As on *Ride the Lightning*, the carnage is prefaced by some acoustic guitar. Opener "Battery" is one of the only traditional thrashers on the album, but even within its relatively straightforward framework there's something more expressive going on. There's a streak of melancholy running through the song that's consistent throughout most of the album, and even though it doesn't water anything down, it can't be ignored either.

The title track follows, the first of the album's three major epics. A drug lament clocking in at over eight and a half minutes, it goes places *Ride the Lightning* only hinted at, including a middle instrumental section with sophisticated textures found nowhere else in the Megaforce catalog.

The idea behind "The Thing That Should Not Be" was probably to darken the mood, but it doesn't work. Instead it's a six-minute walking tour of a single chromatic riff. It's easily the biggest waste of vinyl on the record, and without it, side one would still have exceeded twenty minutes.

Side one closes with "Welcome Home (Sanitarium)," a legitimately moving piece. Its lyrical depiction of madness and isolation is far beyond what the average twenty-three-year-old headbanger would express, and it's easy to see legions of pimply kids hearing it and feeling like their lives were being described to a T. Kirk Hammett really shines, particularly in the sections between chorus and verse.

Side two opens with the record's second epic, "Disposable Heroes." Another track stretching past the eight-minute mark, it's the tale of a soldier who is clearly about to get his ass shot off and an almost perfect distillation of every twist and turn that the group would take on their next LP. . . . *And Justice for All*. Despite its length and girth, it never outlasts its welcome, nor does its follow-up, "Leper Messiah." A brilliant song that has been almost completely overlooked in the Metallica canon, it's a midtempo chug with an impressive double-bass section that "One" could have been written to outdo.

The instrumental "Orion" is the album's third and final epic. It's quite simply light-years beyond anything any of the band's contemporaries could have imagined, much less attempted. The money shot is its middle section, a laidback galactic stonergasm that exits the earth's atmosphere via Thin Lizzy harmonized guitars and Cliff Burton's bass solos. This kind of narcotized boundary pushing would never show up on another Metallica album, and it's tempting to believe that Burton took it with him when he died.

The album wraps up with "Damage, Inc.," a standard thrasher that seems sort of phoned in after the experimental flights of fancy on "Orion," and with that, Metallica's Burton era comes to an end. They would achieve greater commercial success and sell out larger venues, but they would never sound the same again. Whether it was a sound that needed to be abandoned for the band to grow or a lofty peak that they should never have climbed off of will probably be debated by fans until the apocalypse.

MASTER OF PUPPETS

MASTER OF PUPPETS

by Daniel Bukszpan

drum sound. The album demands this sort of shit, man, and we know it'll make the difference."

Finally, the album's "For Whom the Bell Tolls"–like contribution arrives through a pair of doom propositions: "The Thing That Should Not Be" and "Leper Messiah," both demonstrating the dry, uncompromising power-chording taken to even further hardcore extremes by the band's East Coast doppelgangers, Anthrax.

"*Master of Puppets*, in some way, is probably the most concise one of the first four [albums]," figured Ulrich, years later. "With *Lightning*, we were starting to shape our sound. With *Justice*, we took it too far. But *Master of Puppets* is the most concise of those, for better or worse. To have it considered number one [in *The Top 500 Heavy Metal Albums of All Time*] is obviously a pretty amazing thing. I have a lot of respect for that record. It's difficult for me to rate them. I can't say that *Master of Puppets* is better or worse than any of those records. They each are completely their own thing. *Master of Puppets* is obviously the record where it started breaking. When I think of that record, I'll always think of the Ozzy tour, the stage set with the crosses. I'll always think of Cliff. Anytime anybody asks me about records there's all these memories that come into play."

"And you know, I know this is like the oldest cliché in the book, but those records become time capsules;

they become mile markers of your past. When I think of that record, I think of being in Denmark drinking Danish beer, all this shit [laughs], recording at Sweet Silence. I realize now, sort of two-thirds of the way through making a new record . . . we sat around today with our manager and talked about a bunch of stuff and it's really hard to objectify or be objective about our own stuff. I let other people rant and rave about the merits of the records and give opinions, but I have to say that [*Master of Puppets* is] a record that I'm incredibly proud of. It seemed to just sort of come together. We were honing it on *Lightning*, and *Puppets* came the closest to a bull's-eye for that type of stuff. And then on *Justice*, I think it became too bloated and too introverted."

Contrasting specifically the production job on *Lightning* versus that on *Puppets*, Ulrich says that "both of those are recorded at the same place but mixed by different people. I think I might like the mixing on *Ride the Lightning* a little better. I thought on *Master of Puppets* the mixing was a little . . . there's a lot of reverb on a lot of things. Sometimes I think it sounds a little watered-down. But I think the performances are better on that album. On *Master of Puppets*, we had our chops together a little more and we were a little more rehearsed. On *Ride the Lightning*, we were more like writing in the studios where we were recording it. Things like 'For Whom the

Capitol Theatre, Passaic, New Jersey. *Frank White collection*

Felt Forum, New York City. *Frank White collection*

Damage Inc. tour program and tee featuring Pushead art. *All www.WycoVintage.com*

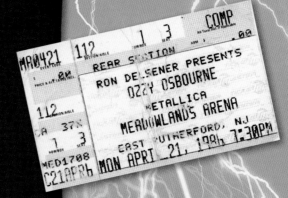

Damage Inc. tour ads.
Author collection

Music for Nations ad, September
1986, U.K. *Author collection*

Bell Tolls' are quite difficult for me to listen to, especially for the drums and stuff. I can hear the tentativeness in the drumming. When I hear it now, I somewhat cringe [laughs]. We wrote it like the day before or something like that."

Issued in February 1986, the album was certified gold eight months later, arguably making *Master of Puppets* the first truly extreme album to hit that plateau signifying U.S. sales of five hundred thousand units. By 2003, the album was an astounding six-times platinum. Upon release, the record stayed on the *Billboard* charts for seventy-two weeks, achieving a chart high of No. 29.

The band was also starting to see its first wave of prominent press. Speaking with *Hit Parader*'s Andy Secher for a full feature on the band's new record, Ulrich defended the record's varied dimensions, explaining, "What I don't like is the people who are trying to lock us into a particular style or sound. We try a lot of different things. Even in the same songs, we're trying two or three different things. That's what makes Metallica special. We're not satisfied to just do one thing well. We're always looking for new ways of playing heavy metal. We toured with W.A.S.P. last year, and while we could dig where they were coming from, we knew it was from a very different place than Metallica. We are not here to say that anything like that is good or bad—it's just different."

As for titling the band's third album, Ulrich said, "We just had a bunch of tunes together, and the name that stood out for us as the album title was *Master of Puppets*. There really isn't any deep meaning to it. It has a mysterious sound to it, but that's about the only special quality it has. Four of the songs on the album deal with the subject of manipulating people, how sometimes you think you're free, but you're really not. But that just happened naturally. *Master of Puppets* is definitely not a concept album of any sort."

Touring for the record found the band opting for eyeballs rather than packed clubs or theaters—that is, opening for Ozzy Osbourne in hockey barns. "The toughest part for us was making sure we had a real happening set," said Hetfield at the time. "Because we're opening for Ozzy Osborne on this tour, we only have about forty-five minutes out there, and we wanted to make sure we had everything just the way we wanted it. We wanted to really communicate what this band's about. We only play seven songs during our set, so it's got to be something of an introduction to Metallica to show everyone what we are capable of doing."

Along the tour trail, Hetfield busted up his wrist goofing around on a skateboard. Still able to sing, he had his guitar tech John Marshall churn out his guitar parts (a role Marshall would reprise in 1992 while Hetfield recovered from a pyrotechnics mishap). In 1989, Marshall would join Metal Church in time for the band's masterful *Blessing in Disguise* album, but his acclimatization to that band came earlier when Metal Church joined Metallica as warmup act after they outgrew Ozzy and started to promote *Master of Puppets* as a headliner.

Then on September 27, 1986, while on the so-called Damage Inc. Tour in Sweden, Metallica's tour bus apparently hit a patch of ice and overturned. Although Hetfield, Ulrich, and Hammett were only a little shaken up, Cliff Burton, who had been sleeping in Kirk's bunk, was thrown from the bus, which then landed on top of him, killing him. Did the bus, in fact, hit ice? Investigators, as well as Hetfield, right there at the scene, could not find any. Hetfield at one point thought the driver might have been drunk, and it was said that the skid pattern was consistent with someone falling asleep at the wheel. It was later determined that the driver was not at fault.

Author collection

Burton's death affected Hetfield most deeply. He got through the experience by recalling his Christian Science roots, which more or less posited that there was no need for dramatic funerals because loved ones live on in their survivors. Metallica proceeded to audition approximately forty bass players (Ulrich claims sixty), then a final four after longtime friend Joey Vera turned down the job, vowing to stay faithful to Armored Saint. Enter one Jason Newsted, of Flotsam & Jetsam fame.

"So we signed Flotsam and the record did really well and of course the horrible thing happened with Cliff," explains Brian Slagel, strangely on the spot to help out with bassists once again. "So Lars called me maybe three or four weeks after that happened, and said, you know, we need a bass player. And I said, 'Well, I hate to do this to myself, but I have your bass player, the perfect guy for you in this band that we have, Flotsam & Jetsam, Jason Newsted, awesome bass player, great guy, perfect musically—he's your guy.' So he was like, 'Okay, send me a tape and we'll get in touch with him' and stuff. Because the first guy that everybody thought of was Joey Vera. . . . Lars called him up first and Joey said, 'I'm not really interested.' Because at the time, Armored Saint was still pretty big. They had done a couple records on Chrysalis and the two bands were almost somewhat at the same level. I mean, Metallica was probably a little bit higher up. But for example, when they played L.A. on the last tour that Cliff did with Metallica, Armored Saint headlined over Metallica at the Palladium, so they were still kind of bigger. So Joey passed on it."

"I don't understand how anyone who knows what this band is about could honestly think that we'd give up," said Ulrich, speaking with the U.K.'s *Sounds*, on the subject of keeping the Metallica machine alive despite the tragic circumstance. "The question was not, 'Are we going to pack it in or not?' It was, 'How fast can we get the whole thing back on its feet again?' Because I know first of all, Cliff would be the first one to get pissed off if we sat around and cried and whined and shit. Secondly, with all

The $5.98 EP: Garage Days Re-Revisited, released August 21, 1987 in the U.S.

"The *Garage Days* record didn't mean anything; it was a punk record—that was the mentality: 'Not-so-produced by Metallica.' That was the whole deal, warts and all."
—*Jason Newsted*

www.WycoVintage.com

www.WycoVintage.com

Cliff 'Em All was a video
retrospective released in 1987
as a tribute to the late Burton.

due respect to Cliff, it's like history—there's nothing we can do about it. For the five years that we've been doing this, Metallica's always been about fighting against all the shit that's been in our way. Something always comes up and we always push on. Cliff was the strongest of the four of us emotionally, and if he saw us sit around and feel sorry for ourselves for the next year on a couch in San Francisco, he'd get pissed off. I know that he'd come around and kick us in the ass and tell us to get back out on the road and continue where we left off."

"I think everyone knew without even saying it to each other," continued Ulrich. "It was just a matter of getting it out in the open. We had a meeting between the three of us and our management. We decided that evening, which was the night before Cliff's funeral, that we wanted to start as fast as we could. So we left the Japanese dates in the itinerary because we thought if we left them in—they were only about five weeks ahead—then that would give us the pressure of getting our shit together in a hurry so we wouldn't just sit around for six months."

Newsted, same age as the rest of the band and originally from Battle Creek, Michigan, joined in time to debut on the *Garage Days Re-Revisited* covers EP (issued August 1987), cranking out rudimentary yet well-recorded versions of songs by Diamond Head, Holocaust, Killing Joke, Budgie, and Misfits. The idea was to test out the band's newly constructed rehearsal and recording space and to take a pause while Hetfield recovered from a second skateboarding accident, this one scotching a scheduled appearance on *Saturday Night Live*. Laughs Ulrich, "Let me just say that before James had that accident, we were asked to go easy on things like that. So you can see how much *that* helped. I don't need a skateboard to fuck myself up—I just need a drink!"

Garage Days would mark the start of a fourteen-year trip on the Metallica machine for the uncompromisingly heavy metal Newsted, one that would provide him substantial financial wealth, along with more than a few resentments and regrets.

www.WycoVintage.com

5.
UNCHAIN YOUR BRAIN
1988—1989

"The vibe this time is so much more urgent, especially with *this* guy. Without saying that we were getting tired or stale before, I think, with this firecracker in the band, the eagerness and excitement has spilled over on everyone else. So we're thinking, let's get on with it, rather than go to the Bahamas for eight months. We are not *that* old yet."
—Lars Ulrich, *Sounds*, 1987

Jason Newsted entered Metallica's world with a healthy respect for what Cliff Burton had accomplished with the band, not only as a cowriter, but also as "the teacher of harmonies and music theory and stuff like that that goes way farther than just putting some chord structures together. Cliff, when he went on tour and walked around, he carried a guitar and not a bass. Thin Lizzy was his god, and all of the harmonies that Phil created and that the guitar players created in that band, those types of things. Between R.E.M.'s harmonies and the ways that they structured music and the theory, and the Thin Lizzy stuff—that was Cliff's building blocks. That was his basis for everything, as far as the really cool music goes, the instrumental stuff like 'Orion,' the somewhat classically tinged things that he did for Metallica. When the stuff seemed to have soundscapes rather than just a one-dimensional wall of metal—that was the difference in the writing. Look on the albums and see, and listen to the record before you look at the credits, and you'll say, oh, that song is very open and big-stringed—the possibilities in that . . . that song will have Burton in there somewhere. And when you hear 'chuka, chuka, chuka,' that's Hetfield [laughs]."

With the enthusiastic new bassist. *Hulton Archive/Getty Images*

Monsters of Rock, JFK Stadium, Philadelphia, June 11, 1988. © Bob Leafe

The next order of business for Newsted was his first studio album of new material with Metallica, the result being a double-vinyl labyrinth of a record issued on August 25, 1988, called . . . *And Justice for All*. As the title suggests, grist for the lyrics came from the politics of the day, Ulrich famously calling this the band's "CNN years." But it's the music and the record's production that stand out, indeed sticking in the craw of Metallica fans, most of whom consider the record somewhat of a love it/hate it affair. *Justice*'s songs are a tangle of technical parts— many tangles, actually—resulting in long and belabored compositions that are then rendered and marinated in a highly eccentric production style quite bereft of bass— neither frequency, nor articulation—which of course was the domain of the new guy, who later intimated that he was somewhat bled out of the final mix.

Lars cools off the masses, Monsters of Rock, Rice Stadium, Houston, Texas, July 2, 1988. *Michael Ochs Archives/Getty Images*

"It was always getting a little more progressive no matter what, when you think about what came before it," begins Newsted. "I think there was something to prove after the *Master* thing went so big. They went out with Ozzy, did all that stuff, and they had something where they really wanted to go fast. There was something they had to prove around their capabilities as being *that* band, the band that can do things that other bands can't, set the standard for speed and convoluted-ness [laughs]. If you think about it, though, relate *Ride the Lightning*'s fastest songs to the . . . *And Justice* fast songs, and you'll see a lot of similarities. James' writing of fast songs, without Cliff, is the same on *Ride* and on

Monsters of Rock, Rice Stadium, Houston, Texas, July 2, 1988. *Time & Life Pictures/Getty Images*

Justice, so those things were already there. He was already heading in that direction."

"Each of the nine songs has completely different ideas and are strong enough to stand up on their own," Ulrich told *Metal Hammer*'s Chris Welch. "It is a fairly long record, but we have not done that because it is the current trend. Metallica always try to avoid trends, and I know it is considered cool at the moment to make long albums. This is not a concept LP, although it lasts one hour and five minutes. As you know, we like to play fast and out there, and we also like to play slow, melodic stuff and midtempo crunch, and heavy, grinding things. We are not painting ourselves into a corner. People see us as a speed band, but we like to play in these different ways. We control things and sometimes slow down. These new Metallica songs are a little leaner, sharper, and have less excess weight—less excess baggage! I suppose the fastest number is 'Dyers Eve.' The title is a bit of wordplay. Thrash? I don't like to use that word. But yeah, we still play fast."

As for the band's approach to writing, "Most of it comes from all our ideas," Ulrich continued. "When we have tried to sit down and write together as teams, it has never worked. But James and I got our stuff together, with skeletal ideas put on tapes, which the other guys hear and add their own ideas. We go from there. James does all the lyrics. Most of the song titles come from all of us."

Quite a different record might have resulted had the band persevered with initial producer Mike Clink, who had been riding high off his work on Guns N' Roses' *Appetite for Destruction* album. However, the relationship broke down and his credit became just a couple of drum tracks. The band was back with Flemming Rasmussen for a third time, but recording in L.A. for much of the first half of 1988. The controversial mix would take place in June at Bearsville, New York, with Michael Barbiero and Steve Thompson presiding. The result is on shocking display on album opener "Blackened," which instantly sets the mood for an almost Voivod-ian vibe, thrash as minimal and yet at maximum, rhythms switching back, no truck to commerciality here.

"James and I were in my apartment in San Pablo, California, a little apartment I lived in when I first got the gig with Metallica," recalls Newsted

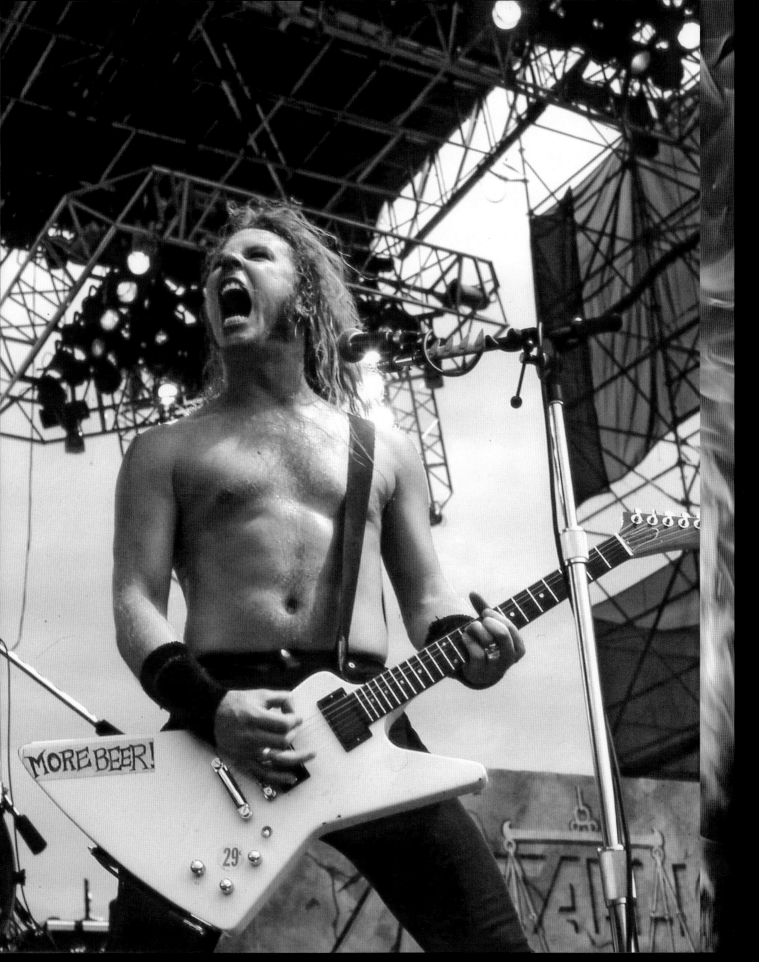

MORE BEER!

Monsters of Rock, Cotton Bowl, Dallas, Texas, July 3, 1988. *Frank White photo*

Irvine Meadows Amphitheatre, Irvine, California, September 22, 1989. *© Kevin Estrada/www.kevinestrada.com*

While Metallica's fourth album is certainly less melodic than its predecessors, it's also more direct and forceful, as well as intriguing, given the layered guitars, tempo shifts, and song structures. The band had clearly become more confident and had matured as musicians since the release of their debut, which was good, because after the death of Cliff Burton, probably the most musical member of the band, two years prior, Metallica had to deliver the goods.

The band emerged from One on One Recording Studios in L.A. on May 1, 1988, armed with an album that would divide their fanbase with its cold production and complex musicianship. It is more aligned with progressive metal than thrash. However, others would hail . . . And Justice for All as the band's masterwork.

AND JUSTICE FOR ALL

by Neil Daniels

Although Justice is not a concept album, there are consistent themes rippling throughout its nine lengthy tracks. Perhaps inspired by futuristic novels such as George Orwell's 1984, these include topics of political, legal, and social injustice in a world of censorship, war, and nuclear weapons. Metallica had become so popular with a generation that they could write and say what they wanted to and the kids would probably take it literally. Even so, the songs are not quite as engaging as those on its predecessor, Master of Puppets, though much of the guitar work is exemplary, such as that heard on the six-minute opening track "Blackened" and the equally lengthy "Eye of the Beholder."

Also on the musicianship front, many fans took note of the double-bass drum sound on the fourth track, "One." Fast, fierce, and aggressive, Lars Ulrich's attack often made best use of simplified drumbeats and a double-bass technique that many metal drummers of the 1980s and subsequent decades would adopt. "One" has also become one of the band's most recognized songs, and deservedly so. It begins slowly, marked by an intricate Kirk Hammett guitar part loaded with hammer-ons and pull-offs, before picking up tempo and commencing a full-on metal assault. Hammett's solo and exchange with James Hetfield are also stunning, but the song was perhaps best known for its video, the band's first, a black-and-white mashup of performance footage spliced with scenes from the film adaptation of Dalton Trumbo's Johnny Got His Gun

After recording, the band hit the road for the Monsters of Rock tour with Van Halen, forcing Ulrich and Hetfield to fly back and forth to Bearsville, New York, for mixing, a situation that proved very tiring for the duo. Perhaps that's why, although it remains Metallica's most progressive album, Justice often lacks the same power, the same guttural kick, as its predecessors. That said, it does have profound moments of absolute metal genius, including standout tracks like the aforementioned "One," as well as "To Live Is to Die." The latter song was written in tribute to Cliff Burton and uses riffs by the late bassist that had not previously been allocated to other songs. The mostly instrumental track is just under ten minutes long and remains the band's only instrumental track featuring Jason Newsted on bass.

Fans had waited two and a half years for a new album, but the band had dealt with a lot before getting there. Finally released in August 1988, Justice became the band's first Top 10 album in the United States. Critical response was almost entirely positive, and while many seasoned fans preferred the first three releases, . . . And Justice for All certainly made a lasting impression on the metal scene. In many respects it ended the first era of the band's career. With a hit album had Metallica now become a mainstream band?

on the origins of this popular *Justice* track, the only one on the album for which he gets a credit. "He came over, I had a four-track machine in my room, in the bedroom actually [laughs]. And there was a Damage Inc. poster right over that thing. I remember that, so I was pretty much into it, you know? And I came up with that original riff, that really fast, kind of off-kilter thing. And then he caught onto that and I know we taped it that day on the four-track, the main bits of that.

"And then I think we went to One on One Studio in West Hollywood [*sic*]. We were in between producers. It was really a weird time. We hadn't been into that fancy of a studio before. There were a lot of distractions in Los Angeles, I remember that. I went in with the assistant engineer Toby Wright, who has come to fame now recording Alice in Chains and stuff like that. I remember Toby and I recording in a room, nobody else around. It is different from any of the other sessions we did with Metallica. I had never been into a studio like that. The only way I had ever recorded was the way we recorded with Flotsam. Four days and a thousand dollars or whatever,

ready, go! And then we did the *Garage Days* record the same way, where it was six days and we just pounded it out. And I thought, that's how it went—whatever you play is what you get. There was no ProTools back then or whatever, fixing shit. We just played it."

"Blackened" would do opening duty on most subsequent tour dates for the album, and years later it remains the most effortlessly enjoyable headbanger from the hard-to-love *Justice* record. The title track demonstrated, unfortunately, the band's penchant for cramming way too many riffs into a song, the final assembly weighing in at almost ten minutes. In fact, Hammett has famously talked about playing the song live and watching the front row yawning, with the band looking at each other after the show and vowing never to play it again (which they do, nevertheless). "Eye of the Beholder" found the band executing the new formula to advantage, using only the

Kevin Estrada
collection

84

catchiest of riffs and transitions, a harbinger of things to come with *Death Magnetic*. It was logical, therefore, that this was one of the few *Justice* tracks chosen for live workout during the long period of roadwork in support of the album.

The album's biggest song, however, would be the massive, prog-minded "power ballad" "One," a shocking tale of war and woe with an even more horrific video, the band's first full-on production clip and, in fact, one of the most popular and iconic videos MTV has ever aired. "The Shortest Straw," one of the record's lesser-known tracks, is a midpaced thrasher, again, with parts that don't quite add up.

"Harvester of Sorrow" is perhaps the album's second-most known track, given its launch as a single in the United Kingdom and the fact that it was played live quite regularly. It's sensible, understandable, catchy, and quite old school despite its slow burn. An impressive Pushead illustration graces the single's picture sleeve, which was made all the more exciting with covers of Budgie's "Breadfan" and Diamond Head's "The Prince."

"The Frayed Ends of Sanity" is another epic slog, built of a long succession of riffs, as is quasi-ballad "To Live Is to Die," which finds the late Burton credited for lyrics. "'To Live Is to Die,' God, that was a really heavy thing," recalls Newsted. "Just the whole vibe around the recording, because it was for Cliff, you know? Nobody has really said those words, but it really was, and everybody knew it, without saying it. There was that kind of feeling that was around. It was just very present; you could feel it. I don't know how to explain it. The lyrics were something that Cliff had written down in a notebook somewhere. I think James found them in his belongings or something, or it was something that he had given James earlier before, some kind of exchange. I think Cliff might have twisted the words around from some other famous writer, but James really liked the way that he put it."

The album closes with its shortest track, "Dyers Eve," a 5:12 thrasher featuring some of Ulrich's precision double-bass work coupled with some of Hetfield's fastest signature quick picking on ruthlessly locked-down

Summer 1989. *All John T. Comerford 111 collection/Frank White Photo Agency*

"'To Live Is to Die,' God, that was a really heavy thing."
—Jason Newsted

rhythm. But with that clacky bass drum sound and lack of bass—both in the low end of the rhythm guitars and in the bass guitar itself—the power written into the song only partially emerges.

"It's pretty tough to do a quick answer, but over the years I've been able to think about it, and it's one of my little thorns," begins Newsted, reflecting on one of the eternal questions concerning . . . And Justice for All: why no bass? "When I came into the band, I'd only ever known one process of recording. Flotsam & Jetsam's first album, Doomsday, was recorded and mastered in six days. And we came in and did Garage Days, with Metallica, mixed and mastered, everything, six days. Play in the room together, jam—that's how I learned to record.

"So Metallica didn't have a producer at that time, when I recorded my bass. I recorded the bass with the second engineer, by myself, in the room, all the songs in two days. Just set up my same rig that I recorded the Flotsam album with, and [Garage Days] with, put it in a room, put a little microphone in front of it like I always did, went in the room, turned on the tape, played it, that was it. . . . Then producers got bobbled around; they recorded the rest of the album. I never sat on the album with any kind of producer and had a guy say, 'This frequency's better. Let's check this bass tone. What speaker cabinet sounds better? Which microphone should we use?' anything like that . . . all of the things I was completely ignorant to at twenty-three years old. Had no idea that those things were the things you needed to do in order to make a record.

"And playing-wise, I mirrored pretty much everything that James played. I was completely influenced by that guy, in all aspects of my life. So I wanted to be as good as him and to be able to play everything he played, so I did. So that came across as . . . knowing what I know now about engineering, and listening how things get jumbled, that's what happened. It was that my playing wasn't clean enough in his riffage, and his quick stop/

Ads for U.K. tour dates. *Both author collection*

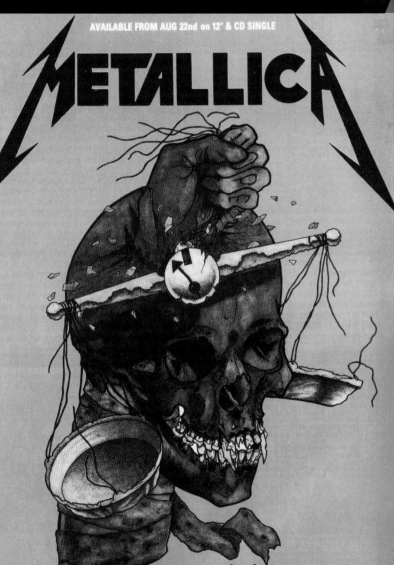

Ads announcing U.K. tour dates and "Harvester of Sorrow" b/w "Breadfan" and "The Prince" 12-inch, and featuring Pushead art. *All author collection*

METALLICA

4 18

DAMAGED JUSTICE

World Tour 88-89
...AND GUEST
OF ALL

METALLICA

DAMAGED JUSTICE

World Tour 88-89
...AND GUEST
OF ALL

Author collection

Hamilton, Ontario, April 8,
1989. *Author collection*

METALLICA

...AND JUSTICE
FOR ALL

METALLICA
DAMAGED JUSTICE

World Tour 88-89
...AND LABOR
ALL

METALLICA
...AND JUSTICE FOR ALL

5447

SEC   ROW   SEAT

GEN. ADM.

AUG. 19, 1989

ADMIT ONE THIS DATE ONLY

BEAVER PRODUCTIONS
PRESENTS
METALLICA
MISSISSIPPI COLISEUM

AUG 19 1989

JACKSON, MS
SATURDAY
8:00 P.M.

NO CAMERAS OR RECORDERS

Author collection

start things and arrangements of the album, that it made his guitar so muddy.

"And the sound is convoluted; it's really fucked to listen to anyway," continues Newsted. "There are a lot of factors that went into that thing. Don't write these as excuses or that shit because I'll be pissed off, because it's not. This is just the facts of how things went. Over the years I've been able to think about it; I tried to reason it out—I had to, because it ate at me. I wanted to know why it would be like that, because people ask me all the fuckin' time, and still to this day, it's what, fourteen years later, and we're still talking about it. So I've had to think about those things.

"Mike Clink came in from Guns N' Roses or whatever, and was there for a week, but nobody sat down for even two hours at a time and said, 'Hey, we're gonna record this,' or called a planning meeting or a production meeting or rehearsals—nothing like that that you do to make an album. None of that stuff was really there.

"So in that pocket, Flemming came in and they finished the record. Then we went on tour with Monsters of Rock in that summer, did the weekend shows, or three or four shows a week, right? Mixed the record at Bearsville in New York and we're doing shows all over the West Coast, whatever. James and Lars are going back and forth from the shows; basically that was the summer where we did all our testing of the waters, the drug consumption and/or all that shit. We were out with Dokken, Van Halen, and Scorpions. Those three bands between them snorted half of Peru in the 1980s. It was really crazy, things that I had never seen before in my life. I was pretty much straight, have some herb every now and then, but I didn't know anything about that kind of shit and I didn't want to. I was there for the metal, man [laughs]. There are some really psycho stories, but you can only talk to me about that when the recorder is not on.

www.WycoVintage.com

Designer: Stu Reid

"But I just want to get the point across that James and Lars are going back and forth, shuffling back and forth to Bearsville trying to figure out who the hell is going to mix the record. So they would go in there totally out of their heads, drive, going there at night, so they have two days of some partial coherence to mix the thing. And the word that I heard after the years went by was that they said to whatever homeboy was mixing it, was get the bass right where you can hear it, and then take it down a dB. So that's the feeling and the mentality.

"The *Garage Days* record didn't mean anything; it was a punk record—that was the mentality: 'Not-so-produced by Metallica.' That was the whole deal, warts and all. The next record was the first Metallica record with the new bass player, Jason. It had to be this thing where psychologically, involuntarily, subconsciously, they had this thing where, 'He is not playing like Cliff. That's not the same kind of shit. He's playing chunka chunka speed metal with the pick, playing the same as James. It's not this brilliant musical 'scape; it's not going to be the same. So let's just get it down here where you can hear the chigga chigga chigga.'

"And also, 1988, starting to taste the fame," notes Newsted. "And you're in front of fifty thousand people, three days a week, starting to taste it, egos are getting going. Anybody, if you've ever been involved in mixing a record . . . I think I can compare it to if you were cowriting an article with somebody and your ideas are the ideas that are good; everybody's ideas are almost as good but not quite as good, so therefore you want to get more of your shit in there. Anybody, you go into the mixing room with them, you sit in there . . . I want you to do a test. You do Monday with the drummer, Tuesday with the guitar player, Thursday with the singer, and you come in the

"And you're in front of fifty thousand people, three days a week, starting to taste it."
—Jason Newsted

AND JUSTICE FOR ALL '89

THEIR MONEY TIPS HER SCALES AGAIN

DAMAGED JUSTICE TOUR '88-'89

SOON YOU'LL PLEASE THEIR APPETITE

All www.WycoVintage.com

mixing room, mix the same song, and you show me the mixes at the end of the day. The singer's day, the vocals will be fucking ripping your face off. The drummer's day, the bass drum will be louder than the vocals. The guitar player's day, the solo will be so fucking loud you won't be able to turn the song up because the frequency will fuck you up. That mentality, along with ego, along with the sorrow, along with the fuckin' [long pause] 'be seen making this scene' producers, the tiredness, the driving, the going on tour, all the combination of things . . . as my short answer [laughs], that is what happened, Martin."

With Jason's insights excellently proffered, one begins to understand. And yet, for all its apparently chaos-caused sonic faults, not to mention its lack of commercial songs, . . . And Justice for All sold well right out of the gate and never stopped selling, vaulting to No. 6 on Billboard and reaching platinum sales almost immediately. In February 1989 . . . And Justice for All was nominated for the inaugural Hard Rock/Metal Performance to be presented at the 31st Grammys. After playing "One" on Grammy night, the first metal band ever to perform on the show, Metallica should have been a shoe-in, but famously lost to Jethro Tull, exposing the charade that is the Grammys.

Touring for the record most notably found the band participating in the preposterous Monsters of Rock package with Kingdom Come, Dokken, and Scorpions, and with Van Halen headlining, stomping through the largest of U.S. venues in June and July 1988.

Afterward, the yearlong Damaged Justice tour found the band sharing stages, variously, with Faith No More, Danzig, Queensryche, and the Cult (much to everyone's surprise, Australian thrashers Mortal Sin supported in their native territory, plus Japan). Always game to proselytize for their unsung heroes, Metallica typically ended their set with a flourish of their beloved obscure metal covers. If these four scruffy metalheads from Thrash Central, California, didn't think it could get any better than this, they would, of course, be proven wrong. But first they would have to forsake the sound that built the band, a career move still heatedly discussed today as the defining point of the long Metallica saga.

All www.WycoVintage.com

6.
SILVER AND GOLD
1990–1995

"Metallica has always been a realistic kind of thing. Few façades and bullshit like that. As long as it's fun and a challenge, we'll keep doing it. What makes it cool is that we try not to get stuck in the same rut. We get bored easily. On the new album, we've taken a bit of a turn. If we did *Justice Part II*, it would be cheating us and everybody else. The minute it becomes an assembly line, it becomes bullshit and we won't be able to get away with it ourselves."
—Lars Ulrich, *US Rocker*, 1991

For their fifth studio LP, Metallica selected ex-Vancouver new waver turned producer/transformer Bob Rock to produce, based on his work on Mötley Crüe's 1989 album, *Dr. Feelgood*. Flemming Rasmussen's production on . . . *And Justice for All* was obscure and interesting, definitely not to everyone's tastes, while the three Metallica records before that had sounded solid and metallic in different ways. This time out, the band wanted to sound anchored and hefty, bulked and less off the handle.

Don't call them "mainstream." Coliseum, Oakland, California, September 24, 1992. *John Storey/Time Life Pictures/Getty Images*

This spread: Nassau Coliseum, Uniondale, New York, December 19, 1991. *All © Bob Leafe*

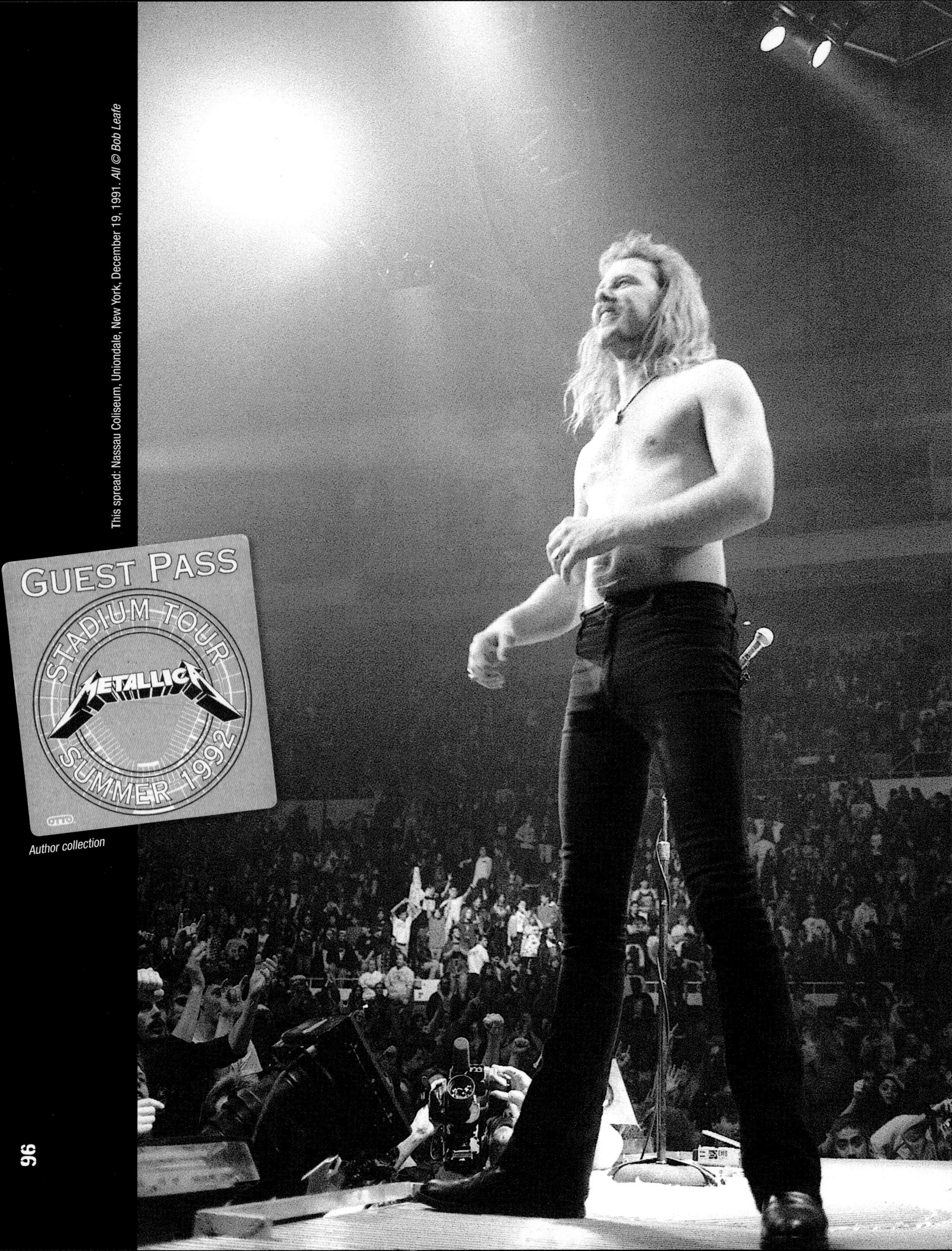

GUEST PASS
STADIUM TOUR
METALLICA
SUMMER 1992
OTTO

Author collection

Indeed, advance single "Enter Sandman" would deliver on this promise of locked-down song. Lovers of the band's past headbanging chuggers, most notably "Escape" and "Seek & Destroy," instantly attached themselves to the strangely anthemic new song—anthemic, but verging uneasily toward nursery rhyme—while those plagued by even doomier dispositions, patrons of "For Whom the Bell Tolls" and "The Thing That Should Not Be," found dark solace in the Sabbatarian trundle of "Sad but True" and "Don't Tread on Me."

"That was a tough one to do," remarks Newsted with respect to "Enter Sandman." "Because when it started to feel like it was going to be something, Bob was really adamant about me keeping things simple and thumping . . . like I did a few little things that were perhaps a little more Geezer-like in the earlier recordings, some of that regular kind of blues box stuff? I mean, in those sessions I learned so much—more in those twenty days than I learned probably in any twenty days, just getting serious about how everything works, how sound actually works going to people's ears. . . . It was so different

from anything else, in terms of how simple we used to keep everything. So that was very interesting in itself. To actually have the downtuning though, to have a nice Spector bass that was sounding so thick and felt so good under my hands, and good headphones that worked, you know, tapped into my head, and I could do whatever I wanted to and it was just there, shaking my whole body. I would always have a subwoofer that I would keep my foot propped up on, so the vibrations would shake all through my bones. I didn't have to have it that loud in the room, but just have the subbies on that you don't really hear, but that you only feel? Just have it coming up through my boots, with my feet right on the sub—stick it up right like that, yeah!"

To experience the magic of the bass like Newsted did, the rapidly growing legions of Metallica fans (three of the band's four past albums had gone platinum by this point) would have to march down to their local CD dispensary, where, on August 12, 1991, they were confronted with nearly solid black album art bearing no title. Five titles

With their statues for Best Metal Performance at the 34th Grammy Awards, Shrine Auditorium, Los Angeles, February 26, 1992. *KMazur/WireImage/Getty Images*

Coliseum, Oakland, California, September 24, 1992. Hetfield jams backstage and wraps the hand he burned in Montreal after straying too close to a flash pot. *Both John Storey/Time Life Pictures/Getty Images*

had been considered, but self-titled was viewed as most consistent with the credo of keeping it simple. "It's a black Metallica logo on a black background," explained Lars at the time. "It's a combination of wanting to get away from the cartoon shit and the silly monster drawings. All these bands and their mascots. I don't want to spend the rest of our careers being associated with some kind of symbol." Thus the Black Album was born, a cheeky contrast to the Beatles' self-titled effort from decades before.

Once inside, the listener was pummeled by songs that were slower, shorter, simpler, and, adjusting for the down-wound directive, rendered bold through boomy and frequency-rich production—production that cost over $1 million and nine months of the band's life through two studios in two different countries. Additionally, the record endured three remixes and, most pointedly, the dissolution of three out of four marriages within the white-knuckled band of warring brothers.

"With this record, one of the first things people say is how natural it sounds," mused Ulrich, just glad to be alive after the ordeal. "Bob has a lot to do with helping us

with some of that goal. One of the first things Bob said to me was how he thought we had a lot more emotion and soul than a lot of people think; he saw that right away. He wanted to make sure that we would not keep that in us, but get ready to let that out. It's just a matter of feeling comfortable and letting that out."

"I think a lot of people that hear the record for the first time might be a bit overwhelmed by the stuff that's there," Ulrich continued. "I mean there are sixty-five minutes, twelve songs. That can be a little overwhelming in one

mouthful. When you hear the whole thing, you might not be able to differentiate as much between each song. But if you take each song and pull it out and listen to it five times before going to the next song, you will hear a lot of things I've been talking about in terms of the simplicity. The overall sheer volume of the thing makes it look like there's a lot of intricate stuff there. It seems to me that when I listen to the record, it's the first time we've made good what we've talked about. A lot of times, we sat down and said let's try some simpler shit, and this time around we did it."

But make no mistake, Ulrich's approach to the drum kit ensured that the songs would go through intense examination from every angle. "Oh, he'll try ten or twelve off them," Hetfield explains when asked about Ulrich's unique approach to end-of-bar fills. "He's not a jamming kind of drummer. It's thought out. You see him on stage and it happens, but yeah, we'll be in the studio, 'Hey, we need some different fills for this thing,'

Arena, Sheffield, England, November 1, 1992. *Giambalvo & Napolitano/ Redferns/Getty Images*

All author collection

Feijenoord Stadion, Rotterdam, Netherlands, June 12, 1993. *Paul Bergen/Redferns/Getty Images*

Author collection

Author collection

METALLICA

THE GOOD
THE BAD & THE LIVE:
THE 6½ YEAR ANNIVERSARY 12" COLLECTI

LIMITED EDITION
RELEASED 7/5/90

Ad for the six-record collection that
included The Six and a Half Year
Anniversary E.P. *Author collection*

"The Unforgiven" b/w "Killing
Time" and "The Unforgiven
(Demo)," U.K. picture disc, 1991.

Day on the Green, San Francisco,
October 12, 1991. The Bill also
featured Queensrÿche and
Soundgarden. *Author collection*

Author collection

and all of us individually are not really confident in our abilities [laughs]. . . . Same thing with drums: 'Oh, let's just jam.' 'Dude, hold on, I've got to figure this thing out.' But once he gets going in the studio, and he builds up some confidence, he'll use up the whole reel of tape."

"I would say that Lars is a manager who also likes to play drums," continues Hetfield. "You know what? He's really, really a great thinker, a great business guy, and he loves playing drums. But he's not the kind of guy who would, you know, on his day off, go and play on his drums. . . . He loves playing drums, and that's what he's done, but I think he's very—how would you say it—he lives in his head a lot. He's a thinker. A big-time thinker.

He will think of ways that people don't play drums and try to do it. . . . It's really math-y for him. He will figure it out, but once he's figured it out, it's unbelievable. He can pretty much play anything if he just puts his mind to it."

With Ulrich's cannon-like drums to the fore, bass—both the instrument and the frequency—was at its most prominent since *Ride the Lightning* some seven years earlier. "There's a lot of personal things involved in that," Newsted later said. "But soundwise, the big step was definitely taken in the Black Album . . . I got heard [laughs]. That was a big deal to me." Newsted had not been happy with his presence, or lack thereof, on the previous record, *. . . And Justice for All,* his first studio LP with the band.

Toronto, November 1991.
Author collection

> **"This time around, I wanted to see if I could get the same energy and aggressiveness without having to hit that snare drum so often."**
>
> **—Lars Ulrich**

All author collection

Still, despite the newly enriched fidelity afforded the band this time out, the overall insistent impression that fans picked up from the Metallica album was its preponderance of slow and mid-paced songs. "This time around, I realize that you can have a really fast guitar riff like on 'Through the Never' or 'Holier Than Thou,'" Ulrich explained, "but if you stick to a midtempo or fast drum thing, not a speed or 'Battery'-type thing, it still has that speed, energy, and aggressiveness. But it has a little more. It has a balance in the swing to it that I don't think our earlier fast songs have had. Some of the songs have really fast guitar pieces, where five or six years ago, I may have stuck a 'Fight Fire' or 'Battery'-type drumbeat on it—gallopy, out-of-control shit."

"This time around, I wanted to see if I could get the same energy and aggressiveness without having to hit that snare drum so often. As a drummer, I got a little bored. I've proved to everybody that I can play, but I don't feel that competitive anymore. There was a time

Metallica's career is divided into two distinct eras: before *Metallica* (a.k.a. the Black Album) and after *Metallica*. The band's twelve-track self-titled set is their Maginot Line, the point where they exploded from cult heroes to multiplatinum juggernaut and their sound broke out of the thrash niche and entered mainstream hard rock, streamlined and accessible but just as gripping and mathematically precise as *Ride the Lightning* and . . . *And Justice for All*. Every track's a winner, and it made Metallica not just metal's best band but one of the best bands on the planet.

It also established a standard by which Metallica would be judged, often unfairly, forevermore.

It didn't come easy. The making of *Metallica* was fraught with infighting among the four band members and with new coproducer Bob Rock, recruited specifically after the group heard his work with Mötley Crüe on *Dr. Feelgood*. But it was a battle of perfectionists who knew that a moment of breakthrough was at hand—if they didn't screw it up— and who were also a tad nervous about taking a path that strayed, at times dramatically, from what had led to that point.

Rock got Metallica to sound like they never had before. He put the four musicians in the studio together rather than recording their parts separately, and he boosted the bottom—particularly Jason Newsted's bass, which had been frustratingly buried in the *Justice* mix— for a more immediate sonic experience that amounted to a knockout punch rather than a flurry of jabs and lightning-quick combinations. Rock also buffed things up with judiciously deployed vocal harmonies, as well as cellos ("The Unforgiven") and orchestrations ("Nothing Else Matters").

Those two songs took Metallica into previously unexplored "ballad" territory, but there was no mistaking them for the sappy love songs that had brought hair bands to the charts. Rather, they are uniquely beautiful, dark, brooding, and intensely personal

METALLICA

by Gary Graff

expressions from frontman James Hetfield, and decidedly more introspective than the sociopolitical tack of *Justice*.

Metallica's rocking tracks took the band in different directions, too. While the group didn't entirely abandon its thrash roots—see "Holier Than Thou," "Don't Tread on Me," "Through the Never," and "The Struggle Within"—they clearly embraced a more measured delivery featuring muscular dynamics and ebb-and-flow drama. Lars Ulrich's drumming, in particular, is much cleaner and Spartan, more Charlie Watts than Neal Peart. It didn't get much better than "Enter Sandman," its slinky, sinewy opening riff exploding into a ferocious but radio-friendly anthem, while "Wherever I May Roam," "Sad but True," "Of Wolf and Man," and "The God That Fails" rode meaty, metallic riffs throughout the songs rather than taking the twists and turns that marked previous releases. "My Friend Misery," *Metallica*'s longest track, wound its way through nearly seven minutes of stomping, dirgey changeups that left plenty of space for Kirk Hammett's white-hot solos.

Hetfield, meanwhile, took advantage of the newfound sonic space to up his lyrical game. "The God That Failed" grappled with the Christian Science teachings that he felt may have cost his cancer-stricken mother her life. "Enter Sandman" explored insecurities that play out well after youth, while "Nothing Else Matters" was the kind of love song only Metallica could credibly deliver.

"Boredom sets into the boring mind," Hetfield sings at one point, but that is hardly an issue on *Metallica*. This is the sound of a group going out on a limb, experimenting, and growing, ironically making itself that much more popular in doing so. *Metallica*'s glories, creative and commercial, would not be re-created again, but the LP unquestionably ensured that the band didn't have to simply ride the proverbial lightning again and again.

The Wherever We May Roam tour overlapped with co-headlining dates with Guns N' Roses. *Both author collection*

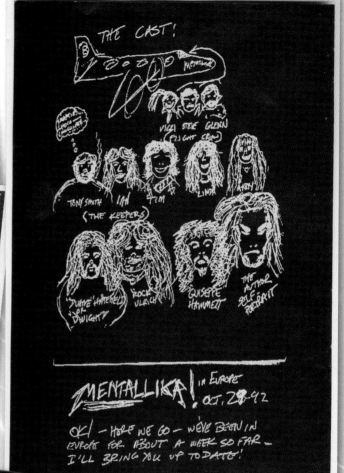

THEY SAID IT WOULD NEVER HAPPEN
GUNS N' ROSES
METALLICA
WITH SPECIAL GUEST
FAITH NO MORE
SUNDAY AUGUST 9 • 5:30PM
EXHIBITION STADIUM
ON SALE NOW
GET YOUR TICKETS AT ALL TICKETMASTER OUTLETS,
OR TO CHARGE CALL THE 24 HOUR TICKETMASTER LINE
870-8000
FOR FURTHER CONCERT DETAILS, CALL CPI'S 24 HOUR CONCERT HOTLINE 538-0088

Both author collection

Issued on November 23, 1993, *Live Shit: Binge & Purge* was a massive multimedia package. *Author collection*

when I felt that I really had to prove myself as a drummer. I think to a certain degree I did, but I don't feel that right now. Right now I feel like kicking back and getting into more of what we're doing than trying to prove myself as a drummer. It's a lot more of a relaxed and comfortable attitude, just sitting back there and driving those songs, without having to take control of them. . . . It's like heavy melody. I think the misconception about melody is that you always associate something nice and happy with melody. A lot of our songs are pretty melodic, but they are heavy in their overall feel. Take a song like 'Nothing Else Matters.' You don't need to have a crunchy, fucking thick Hetfield guitar to be heavy. That's a perfect example of a song that's heavy in feel, but not the playing of it. There's a lot of different ways of being heavy and we keep exploring them. The old myths about the faster you play, the heavier you are went out the window around 1984, around *Ride the Lightning*."

L.A. doppelgangers Slayer famously jumped down Metallica's throats for going mainstream, but Anthrax's

Scott Ian says, with the benefit of twenty years of hindsight, "I loved the Black Album. You know, I had already grown up. I had grown up out of the 'Kill Posers' phase of my life, and only listening to one kind of music. I mean, look, granted, it's funny, because through that whole period of time I was just as much into hip-hop, obviously, if anyone knows our history, as I was into thrash or hardcore. It was the open-minded thing, not being bound by the four small walls of thrash metal, and God forbid if you ever stray outside of those walls or you'll be called a sellout. By the time the Black Album came out, to me, it's just a metal record. It didn't matter anymore whether or not it sounded like *Kill 'Em All*. I wouldn't expect a band on their fifth album to sound like their first album. That might work for certain bands, where they can make the same record over and over again for twenty years, but a band like Metallica, if you listen to Metallica, you hear the differences in their first five albums. They didn't make the same record. So I never had a problem with the Black Album. If anything,

Both author collection

"I loved the Black Album. You know, I had already grown up."

—*Scott Ian*

Toronto, 1994. *Author collection*

Author collection

I had more of a problem with *Justice*, because I hated the production—loved the songs, not the production. . . . But to me the Black Album was the best of both worlds because it sounded incredible and I love the songs."

"James wanted to sing, I guess," Ulrich laughed at the time, commenting on Hetfield's growing vocal prowess as evidenced on "Nothing Else Matters." "I've always known he had that shit buried in him, but I think it was just a matter of timing and it felt like the right time to get some of that out. That song itself came up after a few shows we did last year after an eight-month holiday. After these European gigs, James gave me this tape of all his new ideas. I went back to Copenhagen and I just sat and listened to what he came up with, and that was one thing that really stuck out. When I met up with him the next week at home, I said, 'We gotta fuckin' write this song!' It hit us right away, and it seems to hit everybody else too. Bob really felt that James was a great singer. And James had always been underrated, being more of a front man than a singer. Bob really wanted to bring some of that shit out of James, tried to get him to prove himself as a first-rate singer instead of the guy that can just stand there and growl and look like he wants to kill your family."

But it still needed more, said Ulrich. "We were sitting there with this song, 'Nothing Else Matters,' and we were just looking at each other saying that it was only ninety percent there—it needed something else," he said. "Bob suggested that we use string arrangements, and we tried to keep an open mind so we kind of went for it. But renting a keyboardist and having a guy playing string arrangements on a fucking synthesizer didn't seem right. If you're going to go for it, you gotta go for it all the way. Bob suggested this guy Michael Kamen, who's done orchestral arrangements for Pink Floyd and a lot of movie soundtracks. We sent the tape over to him, and two weeks later he came back and he put a fucking thirty-piece orchestra on there playing our song. It was a little over the top, so we had to tone it down. We just had to maintain a balance to what was originally written. I just wish I could've seen it—thirty fucking guys in a symphony orchestra playing a Metallica song!"

The dirge-like yet elegiac "Nothing Else Matters" would be one of six singles on *Metallica*, propelling the album to 25 million in sales around the world and an astounding fifteen-times platinum by late 2009. The other most enduring

Author collection

© *Rock 'N' Roll Comics No.42, Revolutionary
Comics. Courtesy Jay Allen Sanford*

tracks are introductory single "Enter Sandman" and "The Unforgiven," an oppressive, claustrophobic ballad that nonetheless demonstrated the band's deft skill at exposing the beauty within the funeral.

Metallica would tour the Black Album relentlessly, first hitting Monsters of Rock for the band's fourth time, then embarking on a conventional trek, dubbed the Wherever We May Roam tour, which overlapped with coheadlining dates with Guns N' Roses. In Montreal on August 8, 1992, during a performance of "Fade to Black," James was severely burned during a pyrotechnics mishap. He sang through the rest of the tour, while ex–Metal Church guitarist and current guitar tech John Marshall filled in for the quickest right hand in the west. Post-GN'R, the dates dragged on, with the next leg amusingly called the Nowhere Else to Roam tour. With dates recorded for the massive *Live Shit: Binge & Purge* live box set, the final leg in support of the Black Album would be called the Shit Hits the Sheds tour, its penultimate moment being a stand at Woodstock '94 before a crowd of 350,000.

"James had always been underrated, being more of a front man than a singer. Bob really wanted to bring some of that shit out of James, tried to get him to prove himself."

—Lars Ulrich

All www.WycoVintage.com

"I think that we're pretty good at maintaining an intimacy with our audience," reflected Ulrich. "Every kind of gig you have to approach differently. I think we're getting a feel of how to take care of an arena, without sounding snobby about it. We still like to go back and play club shows. What I don't like about arenas is the sameness every day. When you play forty-five cement arenas around North America, you find it difficult to tell them apart. I think it's all down to your attitude, though. I don't consider ourselves much different than what we've been before in terms of our relationship with our fans. The numbers are bigger. I think sometimes people make that stuff up in their minds a little, saying, 'Now the band is too big and inaccessible.' We're just as easy to get a hold of as we've always been. Most of our fans have a really relaxed approach to us because we're easygoing people. With us, it's like, 'Here are the drunken slobs Metallica again!'

"I'm fucking more hungry," continued Ulrich, long known as the driving force behind the band's ambitions. "I want to get this shit to as many people as possible. I'm more vibed and enthusiastic than I can ever remember being before. It's got nothing to do with how many thousands of square feet my house is, or how fucking fast my car can drive. I'm not doing anything different with my money than any other twenty-seven-year-old kid would do with a shitload of money. One of the bizarre things that happens when you sell records is that they start giving you all this money. We are more comfortable, but it doesn't have shit to do with how we play or anything else. Our feet are firmly on the ground."

7.
AIN'T NO FIT PLACE
1996–1998

"Lars in particular is biting at the bit to get back to work. He eats, sleeps and breathes Metallica! I don't think he enjoys his time away from the band. I've actually enjoyed our break, but I'm also looking forward to seeing what this band will come up with next. We opened so many doors with the last album. Working with Bob Rock really made us reach our full potential. I don't really have any idea when the next album will be ready to go, but I can promise it will be very interesting."
—Jason Newsted, *Brave Words & Bloody Knuckles*, 1994

A huge pile of reckoning and reflection took place in the Metallica camp after the Black Album's blowup success. Hard touring gave way to a spotty schedule of insanely large and memorable festival dates, along with quite a bit of rest and recreation, really for the first time in the band's career. At various points along this extended and colorful touring period, Glenn Danzig and Rob Halford, along with members of Suicidal Tendencies, Diamond Head, and Anti-Nowhere League (lead singer Animal being the penner of "So What?"), joined the band on stage. They played a fan club gig at the London Astoria, which they call the best show they ever played, and on September 3, 1995, they played The Molson Ice Polar Beach Party in Tuktoyaktuk, Canada, north of the Arctic Circle, on an ill-fit bill with alt-rockers Hole, Cake, Moist, and Veruca Salt.

Perhaps pondering a stagnating genre. Netherlands, circa 1996. *Michel Linssen/Redferns/Getty Images*

A week after the release of the new album *Load*, the band explored further frontiers with a hometown club gig broadcast live over the still-new Internet. Innovating further, at least back in January 1993, the band took over a Manhattan record store, converting it into a Metalli-store selling only Metallica products. On November 13, 1995, Metallica took the stage at the legendary Whiskey in Los Angeles as The Lemmys and performed seven Motörhead songs as part of a birthday celebration for Mr. Kilimister, L.A. fixture and proto-thrash purveyor.

Interspersed were drugs, piles of money, and family turmoil, all amid a musical climate marked by the decline of metal. Hair metal was dead; grunge and something called "hard alternative" were the going concerns, featuring downtuning, dirty production, and introspective lyrics. (Industrial metal had its fifteen minutes as well.) Arguably, thrash was going nowhere or, more accurately, had reached its peak with the Clash of the Titans tour of 1990 and 1991, featuring three of "the Big Four": Slayer, Megadeth, and Anthrax (Testament in Europe), with thrash-denouncing Metallica abstaining. It seemed all anyone could say with respect to the genre was that it was stagnating, that it was yesterday's news.

Back in the metal ghetto, Metallica was obscenely successful now, but less so on the street, in the hearts and minds of metal fans. Megadeth reached double platinum with their fine *Countdown to Extinction* album, and chatter existed whether Megadeth was now "better" than Metallica, although such speculation was based more on their previous record, *Rust in Peace*. Less in

MTV Video Music Awards rehearsals, Radio City Music Hall, New York City, September 3, 1996. *Jeff Kravitz/FilmMagic/Getty Images*

Hetfield and Ulrich, the former with his "Burnt Elk Skull" ESP, in 1997. *George De Sota/Redferns/Getty Images*

Author collection

question was whether members of Slayer were worthier metal heroes than Metallica—most emphatically said they were, along with the likes of Testament, Overkill, and Machine Head. Then there was the kickass Texan outfit Pantera, who shot to prominence like a bottle rocket (ignoring their four indies) with *Cowboys from Hell* and *Vulgar Display of Power*, clearly demonstrating that fresh, interesting things could be done with heaviness, even if Metallica had admitted to running out of options and potions.

Indeed, with 1996's *Load* and its *ReLoad* sister record the following year, Metallica certainly seemed to side with critics and music fans who declared metal stagnant (most of whom, unlike Metallica, had *always* thought metal was stagnant).

"It's one work," Newsted begins by way of contrasting *Load* and *ReLoad*, which were built together and released separately. "One collective work pretty much, just performed at different times. . . . So as far as the composition and headspace you were in when you composed the songs, it's one work. I haven't heard them for a long time [sighs]. I have never listened to either of those two albums in their entirety in one sitting—ever. And it's kind of a strange thing, I don't think I've ever sat through any Metallica product other than maybe the Black Album; that was the last, where I ever sat and listened to the whole thing. I've never watched any full Metallica video product or listened to any full Metallica

Nynex Arena, Manchester, England, October 15, 1996. *Peter Still/Redferns/Getty Images*

Hetfield with his Ken Lawrence Explorer #1, circa 1998. *George De Sota/Redferns/Getty Images*

AIN'T NO FIT PLACE · 119

Roseland Ballroom, New York City,
November 24, 1998. *Frank White photo*

recording, ever, in one sitting. It's a hard judgment to make, but as far as the honing and the skills and the bass playing and the sensibilities, once again, and knowing what Bob Rock wanted this time . . . *Load* and *ReLoad* are probably better listening-wise, bass frequency–wise than the Black Album."

Load and *ReLoad* most definitely sound good, and regardless of what one thinks of all the meandering rock songs all over the two records, the band managed yet again to create novel and successful productions, with the drums in particular sounding unique and power-packed.

Bob Rock expertly produced once again, but much of the magic is in the mix courtesy of Rock's righthand man, Mike Fraser. "I just try to enhance whatever the band recorded, or try to get the best out of the songs, to the best of my abilities," figures Fraser. "I try not to put a signature on it. I think the band needs to have their identity and not mine. For good rock bands, I like to have pretty bombastic drums. I like to try to get everything in-your-face as much as possible so that it's right there and you can try and hear everything without something just kind of taking over. But the engineer is sort of the go-between between the producer and actually getting it on tape. And I think the engineer is more responsible for the sound. So obviously the producer has say in it, but the engineer is the one that translates it all into reality . . . you give him all the shades of paint and the mixer is the one that actually paints the picture."

Above: With 1996's *Load*, Metallica seemed to side with critics and fans who declared metal stagnant. *Author collection.*

Left: Ad promoting the new release and the backlist, June 1996. *Author collection.*

Ad promoting U.K. tour
dates, October 1996.
Author collection.

Ad promoting *Load*'s second
single, September 1996.
Author collection

spend on it, it does get appreciably better. But at some
point, you've got to say that there's got to be diminishing
returns. There are lots of options, but that's the way they
like to work as well. Let's do twenty versions of each
thing, guitars a little more, or the drums down, bass up,
all these different versions."

It was worth it, because *Load* and *ReLoad* arguably
represent the best balance between high-fidelity and
eccentricity in the entire Metallica catalog, as full-bodied
as the muscular *Metallica* production, but just a bit weird
and intriguing. Most fans and even much of the band now
agree that quite a lot of material on the two records was
substandard (two-thirds of the songs spread over the
albums were recorded at the initial early-'96 sessions).
Still, the openers, "Ain't My Bitch" and "Fuel," were kick-
ass Metallica songs of the new post-*Justice* style.

Load coughed up the single "Until It Sleeps," which
really got the debate going on whether Metallica had lost
the plot, while "2 X 4" offered a Corrosion of Conformity–
like blues metal. "Wasting My Hate" was a solid rocker

"On *Load* and *ReLoad*, Randy Staub and I split mixing
the record," Fraser continues, "just because they wanted
to get it done quicker, and they wanted to spend three or
four days a song, per mix. So if you're looking at fourteen
or sixteen songs, or whatever it was, times three, it's
way too long. So I came in and helped them out. So I
was just, you know, 'Here's bass, drums, and guitars,
and in the next day or two, we'll have vocals for you,
and then on the last day here, we'll have some final drum
edits.' Because they were still doing things and changing
stuff while we were mixing it. So there weren't any band
interactions there for me. I was off in another studio and
they would come in and check my mixes and approve
them, and off they go."

Three and four days for a mix? What could possibly
take so long? "Just taking your time on it, really honing in
on, you know," Fraser explains. "Is this drum exactly the
sound I want, and is this high hat sitting in the right spot?
Are the guitars right? You can easily spend three days.
It's tough, but you can do it. And each hour or so you

Power ballad "Mama Said"
was released as a CD single in
November 1996. *Author collection*

"You can only be what the public thinks you are for so long before it becomes boring," Kirk Hammett said in 1996, adding that since the phenomenal success of the Black Album he had "begun to feel quite objectified." Lars Ulrich was also hungry for change. The rock world had changed in the five years since *Metallica*, their last release. They were no longer competing with Guns N' Roses and Bon Jovi for chart action; they were up against the post-grunge, post-Nirvana offerings of acts such as Pearl Jam and Soundgarden, and Ulrich was determined Metallica would not be left behind in the public mind.

In their determination to save Metallica from post-grunge obsolescence, Ulrich and Hammett combined to create Metallica's boldest, if not always their most likeable, move yet. The result was the most radical and certainly most hotly debated album of the band's career, at least to that point: *Load*. It wasn't that they had left thrash far behind; it was as if they had tried to shrug off the very sound of Metallica itself in a self-conscious reconfiguration that had begun with new shorter haircuts and tattoos, and even makeup and piercings. The music seemed made to match the look: the kind of bluesy, far-out rock 'n' roll that liked to shimmy and shake instead of shatter and explode. "When someone says 'Metallica,' they think heavy metal, thunder, and lightning, long hair, drunk kids," explained Hammett. "But why should we? Why should we conform to some stereotype that's been set way before we ever came into the picture?"

There were a couple of long tracks—"Bleeding Me" at more than eight minutes, and "The Outlaw Torn," clocking in at more than nine—but these were the exceptions. In the studio, the rule of thumb was now to keep things tight and rhythmic, or "greasy" as Ulrich liked to describe

LOAD

by Mick Wall

it. Lyrically, too, James Hetfield had moved on from tales of the Four Horsemen to his most personal and painfully autobiographical material yet—tracks such as "Poor Twisted Me" (*I drown without a sea*); "Thorn Within" (*So point your fingers . . . right at me*); "Bleeding Me" (*I am the beast that feeds the beast*); "Cure" (drug addiction as metaphor for moral sickness); "Ronnie" (based on the real-life Washington, D.C., shootings in 1995 by schoolboy Ron Brown); and "King Nothing" (about the king-size ego Hetfield now saw in his own dressing room mirror).

Mostly, they got it right. "Ain't My Bitch" was a firestorm. Hetfield explained that the "bitch" was a metaphor for a problem and that the point of view was that of someone with no concern for anyone's troubles but his own. Nonetheless, what James later called "the U2 version of Metallica" was a big turnoff for many fans. Even the album sleeve—designed around a detail from a painting entitled *Semen and Blood III* by controversial artist Andres Serrano—seemed designed to get up as many noses as possible.

For Ulrich, however, the logic was obvious. If Metallica could no longer be expected to fulfill the role of outsiders—that job having been taken by the grunge generation—then the least they should do is try to ensure they arose to that pantheon of bands that existed somewhere beyond the conventions of rock fashion. "Now you got U2 and REM . . . and Metallica," he said in 1996. "In America, these borders just don't exist anymore. After Cobain came along, everything became so blurred. Nowadays, bands are just bands: some are harder, some are softer, but heavy metal and pop and this and that . . . it's all just one big fuckin' soup."

ReLoad was the second-stage rocket in Metallica's radical transformation. Released on November 18, 1997, it marked lead guitarist Kirk Hammett's thirty-fifth birthday and, perhaps even more propitiously, came at a time when "metal" was officially a dirty word. "Nirvana's 'Smells Like Teen Spirit' video gave metal the biggest haircut of all," Hammett told me at the time of *ReLoad*'s release. "All of a sudden everyone who was a metalhead was suddenly a grunge guy saying, 'I've always been into this type of music. I hate metal.'"

Including Metallica—something that was made clear when Lars Ulrich announced to the U.K. music press in early 1997 that the band had hung up their heavy-metal spurs. Actually, that point was made the year before when the men in black lopped off their flowing locks, headlined Lollapalooza alongside Soundgarden, and released *Load*, a dark, moody collection that showed a less tightly wound, more introspective side of the thinking fan's metallurgists.

Envisioning a double album, the band wrote twenty-seven songs and recorded drum tracks for most of them before realizing they'd taken on too much. "We were more than nine months into the recording and we weren't even done with half of the songs," Hetfield told me. "We realized it was just too much to do. Too much to swallow."

"We thought it might be asking too much of fans to digest all of that," added Hammett, so the band decided to split the project in two, releasing *Load* in 1996, and *ReLoad* a year later.

The band hired photographer Anton Corbijn to shoot the sleeve pictures for both discs and commissioned a pair of paintings by controversial Cuban-American artist Andres Serrano: *Semen and Blood III* (which Serrano rendered using bovine blood and his own semen) for the cover of *Load* and the similarly executed *Piss & Blood XXVI* for the cover

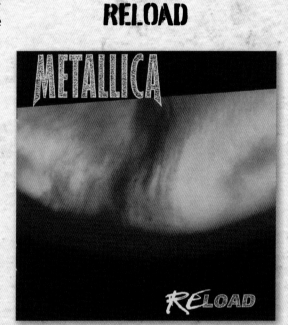

RELOAD

by Jaan Uhelszki

of *ReLoad*. To what ends? Hetfield publicly denounced the decision, telling *Classic Rock* in 2009, "Lars and Kirk were very into abstract art pretending they were gay. I think they knew it bugged me . . . I just went along with the makeup and all of this crazy, stupid shit that they felt they needed to do."

Fans looked askance at the entire package, unable to readily accept this new Metallica. The songs signaled that some Rubicon had been crossed, but the thirteen tracks on *ReLoad* caused a greater uproar, proving that *Load* wasn't just an anomaly. Except for "Fuel," which conjured up the ire, vitriol, and speed of Metallica's early canon, *ReLoad* was a death knell for the particular kind of thrash metal that Metallica had invented, perfected, and then distanced themselves from. Instead of speed, *ReLoad* went for agility and gritty grace, including slowed-down and reflective tunes such as "Unforgiven II," a more fully realized and psychological sequel to its self-castigating predecessor, with a little bit of a country shine on it, and the haunting Hollywood horror story "Memory Remains," equal parts *Sunset Boulevard* and *Whatever Happened to Baby Jane*, and featuring an unnerving duet with a croaking Marianne Faithfull.

But for all the fallout over the paradigm shift, one can't miss that Hetfield's singing had grown by emotional increments. On *ReLoad*, he no longer sounded like he was being pursued by a pack of red-eyed dogs, showing a more human and wounded side, and even taking on some of the sorrow and depth that Layne Staley used to evince with an injured machismo. "I don't think people understand how many different sides we have, how soulful a singer James is," Ulrich explained. "We are not as shallow as most of the people in the world we're seen as inhabiting."

late in the sequence, and "King Nothing" kicked Sabbath-style and was deemed video-worthy, one of four tracks on the album that received controversially artsy clips. At the ass end, both "Ronnie" and "The Outlaw Torn" caused accusations that the band had gone grunge or alternative or at least slowed to a crawl—there's no thrash to speak of on *Load*.

ReLoad's most famous tracks were "The Memory Remains," featuring Marianne Faithfull, and the ponderous ballad "The Unforgiven II." "Better Than You" and "Devil's Dance" were choice rockers, though, and "Slither" was a redo of "Enter Sandman" with grunge-like vocalizing and lyrics. Truth is, there's quite a bit of stomping metal on *ReLoad*, including, late in the sequence, "Prince Charming" and "Attitude," but also a recurring doomy, bluesy, Alice in Chains–like vibe, which was the main source of the denunciations of these two records (notwithstanding the fact that the cover art features stylized pictures of blood, semen, and urine).

With a few years hindsight, Ulrich figures that each record has a unique vibe all its own: "I guess they have taken on different personalities. I was very adamant about forcing this whole thing that they are the same album because they were birthed at the same time. It's one year's worth of writing spread out over two separate records. But at the same time, that's kind of bullshit because they're obviously two separate records—here's one record and here's another one [laughs]. They have different titles, they have different covers, and they have different years, so that's a little thin [laughs]. I mean, *ReLoad* might be just a hair heavier or something, or some of the more experimental stuff was on *Load*."

"I think that after the Black Album," he continues, "we felt that we could experiment and do whatever the fuck we wanted and now we were going to try to do a fucking kind of ZZ Top–ish boogie kind of thing, like 'Poor Twisted Me,' or we could do a kind of weird-ass almost Southern-y, Skynyrd-y kind of thing, a song like 'Ronnie.' So we were proud to once again showcase just some different stuff. And I think there was a point where we felt that we earned a kind of freedom, once again on the Black Album, that we earned the right to do that. And then you can debate whether it worked or not. A lot of people do that [laughs]. But I'm very proud of those records. I'm proud of the dare and I'm proud of the undertaking. You know, I'm proud of all of it—and I have questions with all of it. But ultimately, I'm sort of at

Released in 1997, Mandatory Metallica was the first of a series of radio-only promo CDs. *Author collection*

Author collection

Released November 11, 1997, the lead single from *ReLoad* featured Marianne Faithfull on backing vocals. *Author collection*

peace with everything we've done. And I don't say that with kind of an attitude where I'm going to be protective of everything we've done, like, okay, all the naysayers now, I'm just going to shove it all back in their face. I mean, I'm proud of it because at the time, it was the right thing. And no matter what I think of . . . *And Justice for All* now, or what I think of *ReLoad* now, at that time it was the right thing."

"There was a lot of work put into those records," continues Ulrich, responding to my praise for the production, "and I think the meticulousness and certainly the sounds on songs like 'Devil's Dance,' 'Bleeding Me,' you know, some of that stuff is pretty fucking cool. It was a bit disappointing with *Load* that a lot of people, the way people reacted to the music on *Load* was biased by how some people dealt with the pictures, the hair and all

that crap. I think that a lot of people would come up to me in the years after *Load* and say variations on like, 'I never gave the record its fair chance when it came out, because I could never get beyond Jason Newsted with eyeliner on or whatever,' you know what I mean?

"I think musically there's some pretty strong stuff on there, but I wish some of it, in the way that I'm thinking now, could have been edited out. And some of the songs are on the bloated side. And one of the things we're doing now is that we're trying to be a little leaner. But you know, 'The Outlaw Torn,' some of that shit is pretty fucking awesome. . . Funny thing about living in San Francisco, your neighborhood radio station plays Metallica like every ten minutes. . . . I find myself listening more to the earlier stuff when we're making a new record now because you use a lot of it as a reference point. But *Load/ReLoad* is, I would say, one body of work spread out over two records. That's probably the best way of saying it—the result of one creative spurt."

Load and *ReLoad*, like *Metallica*, both peaked at No. 1, though sales were down compared to the Metalli-monster that ate 1991 (but how could they not be?). Still, *Load* hit a robust five-times platinum, with *ReLoad* achieving four-times platinum and the band getting in a little TV promo with a trip to *Saturday Night Live* in December 1997, where they performed "Fuel" and "The Memory Remains," the latter with guest vocalist Faithfull.

Touring during this period found the band reinforcing

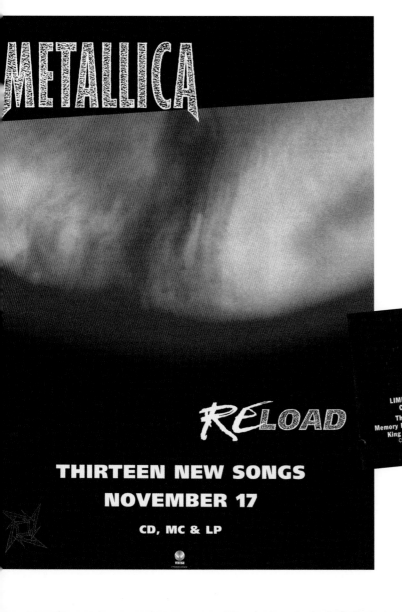

Left: Both *Load* and *ReLoad* sound good, regardless of what one thinks of all the meandering rock songs all over the two records. *Author collection*

Above: *ReLoad* single "Unforgiven II" was a follow-up to *Load*'s "Forgiven" and would be followed by "Unforgiven III" on *Death Magnetic*. *Author collection*

the alternative rock messaging, first signing on to headline Lollapalooza on a bill that included Psychotica, Screaming Trees, Shaolin Monks, Rancid, Ramones, Devo, Cocteau Twins, and Soundgarden. The Poor Touring Me leg found the band supported by old friends Corrosion of Conformity, plus Soundgarden and Korn, while the Poor Re-Touring Me campaign saw them supported by the grunge-lite Days of the New and the grunge-solo Jerry Cantrell.

On November 23, 1993, in the space between *Metallica* and *Load*, the band issued their first live album, a massive multimedia package called *Live Shit: Binge & Purge*. Post-*Load*, on November 24, 1998, Metallica issued what felt like a sister product to the live spread, given the covers all over the third disc of *Binge & Purge*. *Garage Inc.* is anchored by the reissue of the long-out-of-print *Garage Days* EP, while offering a bevy of additional covers from all over the rock (and punk) spectrum, including a Motörhead set, a bunch

of B-sides, and fully eleven new recordings specifically for the twenty-seven-track package. Highlights from an angry metalhead point of view include visits to the church of Sabbath and Mercyful Fate, but the band scored hits with their thundering remakes of Bob Seger's "Turn the Page" and Thin Lizzy's "Whiskey in the Jar." The latter, for which Metallica garnered their fifth Grammy, is bar-none one of the most insanely catchy things you'll ever hear on a Metallica record.

Subsequently, the band embarked on the Garage Remains the Same tour, support coming from Monster Magnet. Guest stars jumping up on stage this time, a regular thing with Metallica, included Phil Anselmo, Kid Rock, and members of Anthrax, Biohazard, and Mercyful Fate. Betwixt dates, the band found time to hobnob with the upper crust, recording twice with classical orchestras, once in Germany and once in New York City, to prepare for the *S&M* experience to come.

Both author collection

Jessica Kartak-Kegley collection

"I think musically there's some pretty strong stuff on there, but I wish some of it, in the way that I'm thinking now, could have been edited out."

—Lars Ulrich

Grabbing a huge chunk of the 1998 holiday season market for greatest hits and compilation packages—yet being anything but opportunistic, fan-exploiting tripe—the *Garage Inc.* covers collection was released on November 28, 1998, a year after the second installment of the polarizing *Load/ReLoad* two-part album cycle was completed.

Everyone seems to remember where they were when Metallica traded their flowing manes for mascara, piercings, and clothes that made them look like quasi-hip owners of mob-run dance clubs or brand-new sushi bars. For an older, established band to pull a "back-to-our-roots" move, especially during such a stretch of career uneasiness, is one of the oldest tricks in the book and, therefore, usually seen as the transparent, dishonest nonsense that it is, at least among those who are paying attention. However, this was not the case with Metallica or *Garage Inc.* In fact, the band had spent the previous fifteen-plus years building a side line covering obscure and not-so-obscure artists that had influenced them to be . . . well, Metallica.

Garage Inc.'s first disc underscores that point, made up of eleven tracks recorded during the previous September and October specifically for this release. And it's knocked-out, down-and-dirty, featuring covers of Nick Cave and the Bad Seeds, Diamond Head, Black Sabbath, Discharge, Thin Lizzy, Bob Seger, Mercyful Fate, Lynyrd Skynyrd, and Blue Öyster Cult.

The second disc, however, is where the band really pays homage to their roots and their record collections. The first half collects reissued content, all of which was well out of print by late 1998, including *The $5.98 E.P.* five-song 12-inch (Diamond Head, Holocaust, Killing Joke, Budgie, and Misfits), the band's first recordings with Jason Newsted, in its entirety. Further covers of Budgie and Diamond Head, as well as Blitzkrieg, Queen, Anti-Nowhere League, and

GARAGE INC.

by Andrew Earles

Sweet Savage, and had turned up as B-sides, as had the four tracks collectively entitled "Motörheadache," covers of one of Metallica's most frequently noted influences.

The double-CD/triple-LP set sold 426,500 copies within a week of release, nabbing the No. 2 slot on the *Billboard* 200, and by 2003 had been certified five-times platinum (2.5 million copies sold). Their cover of Seger's "Turn the Page" gave the band their longest-running No. 1 (eleven consecutive weeks) on *Billboard*'s (Hot) Mainstream Rock chart (it also cracked the Modern Rock chart at No. 39), along with a much-talked-about video—a trailer-park musical drama starring adult film actress Ginger Lynn Baker as a stripper who also prostitutes herself to provide for her child. (Inexplicably Lars Ulrich hadn't heard this ubiquitous slice of classic rock until 1998, when it came on the radio as he drove across the Golden Gate Bridge.) *Garage Inc.* placed two other singles on the (Hot) Mainstream Rock chart: a cover of the Misfits' classic "Die Die My Darling" (No. 26) and a version of Thin Lizzy's appropriation of the Irish traditional folk song "Whiskey in a Jar" (No. 4).

It could be said that Metallica both perfected *and* supremely botched the art of the stopgap gesture. Since 1991's breakthrough Black Album, the band has, after all, had plenty of opportunities to unleash all manner of holdovers. With a music industry anomaly such as Metallica, these albums, documentaries, tour films, festival dates, and less tangible career moves have served multiple purposes to varying degrees of success. At a very basic level, they give fans something to chew on while waiting on the next proper studio album. From a marketing and PR standpoint, they also function as damage repair, like 2012's successful Orion Festival did in the wake of the Lou Reed and Metallica joint effort, *Lulu*. *Garage Inc.*, however, is one of the home runs.

8.
HARMONY DIES
1999–2007

"I still have a wild streak the size of the f***in' Grand Canyon, but I'm still really into monster movies and toys and I still listen to crazy music all the time, but it's just that my tastes are getting wider and more varied. I'm really into art and photography. I like pop art, abstractions, cubism and European symbolism. I'm actually afraid to make a big purchase."
—Kirk Hammett, *Metal Hammer*, 1996

Saddled with the ill reception to *Load* and *ReLoad*, essentially as records that were too laidback, Metallica stepped in it further by recording with an orchestra. The result was tagged with the cheeky title *S&M*, the guys turning in an album two CDs long performed with the San Francisco Symphony as conducted by the esteemed Michael Kamen and featuring two new songs: "No Leaf Clover" and "- Human."

April 2003, a few months before the world would learn about the in-fighting and be presented a weird, impenetrable album. *Mick Hutson/Redferns/Getty Images*

MTV Movie Awards, Sony Pictures Studio, Culver City, California, June 3, 2000. *Frank Micelotta/ImageDirect/Getty Images*

If the final product sounded immensely considered and constructed, Newsted insists that on the part of the band, there was "very little rearrangement. When we dug out the old stuff that we had never performed live before, like 'Ktulu' and stuff, that was moved around a little bit to try to keep the strings in mind. Just those things that we really didn't know. Just like the things they didn't know, those actually turned out to be the better ones [laughs]."

Newsted recalls that the biggest challenge was getting the relative volumes of the parties to sit well together. "Number one challenge by miles," he says. "We didn't have any amps onstage, but we still got all the volume that was coming out of the monitors and the PA and that kind of thing. And these people were playing hollow wooden instruments that will resonate at the drop of a pin. An ant walks on it and it goes rat-tat-tat-tat [laughs]. So when a big bass frequency comes through it and a lady is trying to play [makes a violin sounds], it just goes 'brrrrrrrrr.' It's pretty tough for those people to deal with something that is completely from another planet for them. There's no way they

would have been ready for that. But we got by that and figured out the monitoring system."

"But we came into a situation," continues Newsted, "where the strobe lights on the end of 'One,' for instance, or a song with a lot of staccato riffs, well, the guy would flash the strobes on the music stands, the upright part of the music stands, the tubes, and the music would be on the page, off the page, on the page, off the page, on the page, off the page, white notes, white notes [laughs]. And since these people were four or five years old, they've been taught to play compositions from twelve or sixteen or eighteen composers. And we're played all this shredding stuff and it's like, 'Wait a minute, that's not familiar to me, that's not my style, who is this?' So we were playing the known and they were playing the absolutely unknown. We got beyond those things, because they are so freaking professional. You put the paper in front of them and three times later, they're knocking it out.

"But the one thing you could not prepare them for, ever, is the crowd. So once the kids came in, that was a little different than what they're used to [laughs]. The cats in

Ulrich testifies before the U.S. Senate Judiciary Committee on file sharing as Roger McGuinn looks on. Washington, D.C., July 11, 2000. *Joyce Naltchayan/ AFP/Getty Images*

the ties with their hands in their laps, 'Oh, a smattering of applause.' These kids are going, 'Fuck yeah!' and spitting, but they were well behaved this time. They really were; they watched out for other people, because it was a mixed crowd. There were Metallica fans, but there were some very curious individuals, season-ticket holders that wanted to check it out . . . . But one of the most beautiful experiences ever. The melding of two worlds, instead of the clashing of two worlds. It was incredible that anything sounded like anything, coming out of that. And for it to sound magnificent, I mean, that was really something. Made some good friends during that thing. The principal cellist of those shows is the man that penned all of the string arrangements for my Echobrain album [Jason's

three-record alternative-lite band, the starting of which caused friction with the rest of Metallica]."

Echobrain was Newsted's cool idea to knock off raw EPs with well-regarded underground rockers at his own recording den, The Chophouse. To the bassist, it was like Metallica, once a tight gang, was beginning to have less and less in common. "The Metallica guys started getting money ten years ago or whatever, and whenever that comes along, no matter how strong your pride or your ethics are, it's still going to fuck with you a bit," he explained at the time. "And you start forgetting why you're doing it. And I think that's kind of what happened. The Metallica guys, they just became distracted by other things, families and stuff like that, and they didn't want to

Turner Field, Atlanta, Georgia, July 11, 2003.
Mick Hutson/Redferns/Getty Images

spend as many hours a day playing music, and I *did* want to spend more hours playing music. Now, I've learned my work ethic from Metallica, so don't get that wrong. But that was then. So now there's other things they want to spend their time on and they don't have time to give me eighteen hours anymore."

Ulrich found himself heavily involved in one of those "other things" when he dared to stick up for artists' rights and speak out against music being given away on the Internet. The firestorm was touched off by the discovery that the band's new "I Disappear" song, written for the *Mission: Impossible II* soundtrack, had been leaked. File-sharing site Napster was sued, with Dr. Dre eventually joining Metallica. Light was made of the battle on 2000's MTV Music Video Awards, with both Ulrich and Napster founder Shawn Fanning appearing, though separately. Ulrich was booed as a rich establishment rock star (the year before, the band was among an elite group issued the very first RIAA diamond awards, theirs for sales of

over ten million copies of *Metallica*). In the end, Metallica lost the PR battle but won the war—Napster filed for bankruptcy and was ordered liquidated. Essentially, it was merged out of existence through its affiliation with digital-music subscription service Rhapsody.

With the Napster fallout, Newsted on his way out of the band, and Hetfield plagued by back pain from a jetski accident and a subsequent stint in rehab for alcoholism—and without the distraction of continual touring to fill the gaps—Metallica had almost too much time to be introspective and destructive. The only roadwork around this time was the Summer Sanitarium tour in the summer of 2000, which caused consternation among the faithful, given that the package found Metallica playing with garish nü-metal propositions like Korn, as well as System of a Down and Kid Rock. Still, the band stayed active. Hetfield jumped on stage with both the Misfits and Corrosion of Conformity, as did Hammett with Sammy Hagar. In November 2000 the band performed in the

Rehearsing backstage, Ohio Stadium, Columbus, Ohio, July 19, 2003. *Mick Hutson/Redferns/Getty Images*

On the MTV News Platform with Kurt Loder at the MTV Video Music Awards, Radio City Music Hall, New York City, August 28, 2003. *Mark Mainz/Getty Images*

parking lot at the VH1 Music Awards and Ulrich started a record company, first championing Systematic. In 2001, Ulrich also tried his hand at trivia by appearing on *Who Wants to Be a Millionaire?* and then on radio, taking over KSJO for four hours of DJing in May of that year.

But Hetfield wound up in rehab for more than four months at the end of 2001. Recording of what would become *St. Anger* would have to be put on hold. Not that anybody was getting along: Newsted had left in January, leaving producer Bob Rock to plunk the bass while the guys spun their wheels in finding a replacement for Newsted, who, in addition to citing a number of nuanced and complex personal clashes with his strong-willed mates, chalked his departure up to a bad case of headbanger's neck, which is more prevalent than you might think.

"Nothing—it hasn't changed in a year," Ulrich told me, addressing the bass player situation at the time. "We've made a conscious decision to not even deal with it until the record's done. Bob is playing ninety percent of the bass tracks and James plays a couple of odds and ends here and there and it's awesome. It's just not a part of what's going on right now. When the record's done, we're going to sit down and find a new bass player. And I don't want to get into a Rolling Stones kind of thing where it's three guys and some fucking rent-a-guy. I want to get a new member of Metallica. I just don't want to do it until the record's done. I've got somebody every five minutes telling me, 'Hey, you should get this guy, you should get a famous guy, you should get a new guy, you should get an old guy, you should get a very young guy, you should get a guy with no experience, you should get a guy with experience, get a chick, get a fucking monkey,' you know what I mean?"

More is known about the making of *St. Anger*, issued June 5, 2003, than one could possibly digest. Over one thousand hours of film footage shot of these tense times and the actual sessions were distilled down to one of the most gripping band documentaries ever crafted, *Some Kind of Monster*, released to a tornado of controversy in January 2004.

Download Festival, Glasgow Green, Glasgow, June 2, 2004. © Trinity Mirror/Mirrorpix/Alamy

"When the record's done, we're going to sit down and find a new bass player. I want to get a new member of Metallica. I just don't want to do it until the record's done. "
—*Lars Ulrich*

For good reason, fans were fascinated. Not only did the movie reveal the bitter in-fighting, but also the making of an album considered weird, impenetrable, and negatively affected by what was known as "nü metal," a brief but for a time massive subgenre characterized by downtuning, a lack of guitar solos, a focus on bass and weird bass tones, rap and other urban music nods, and deeply personal lyrics.

St. Anger featured Metallica sampling from all of the above, picking innovative bass lines and sounds, Hetfield lyrics that felt at times like too much information, and a Mudvayne-like drum sound dominated by a ringing

Left: Continental Airlines Arena, East Rutherford, New Jersey, October 22, 2004. *Frank White collection*

Below: Gwinnett Center, Duluth, Georgia, November 13, 2004. *Frank Mullen/ WireImage/Getty Images*

Wembley Stadium, London, July 13, 2007.
Mick Hutson/Redferns/Getty Images

snare. Much of the album is forgotten and was never played live, due partially to the band's admission that the songs were hugely stitched together Frankenstein-like and therefore really, really hard to reproduce.

Highlights from *St. Anger* include opener and single "Frantic," which features one of Metallica's punchiest opening sequences ever. "Some Kind of Monster" and the title track are also direct enough to win fans, while late in the sequence, "The Unnamed Feeling" is doomy but somehow catchy and demonstrative of the album's innovative, crushing production, Metallica adding to their bulging collection of smart, strange production palettes with guttural bass, carnal guitars, and perennial cymbals all fighting for space in the mix. Elsewhere, "Dirty Window" is a welcome semitraditional thrasher, while "Invisible Kid" is an unsung utilitarian rocker that could have been a performing single.

At Neil Young's Bridge School Benefit Concert, Shoreline Amphitheatre, Mountain View, California, October 28 2007. *Anthony Pidgeon/Redferns/Getty Images*

Flyer for Eurock festival at Lac de Malsaucy near Belfort, France. *Author collection*

Dynamo festival flyers, Mierlo, Netherlands. *Both author collection*

Big Day Out, Buckinghamshire, England. Metallica played a number of European festival dates in the summer of 1999. Ben Harper was an interesting booking on this bill. *Author collection*

After driving a stake into their restless experimentations of '90s—whether the southern rock love letters of *Load* and *ReLoad*, or taking their canon to the symphony on *S&M*—Metallica put their sonic recalibrations behind them on *St. Anger* and returned to the raw, vitriolic savagery of their earlier work, using 1984's *Ride the Lightning* as a bread crumb trail back to the days when they were the kings of speed metal. "I was always really scared of going back," Lars Ulrich confessed at the time of *St. Anger*'s release. "So, okay, after fifteen years, why go back *there*?"

After the release of *Load*, Ulrich vowed that the band would release a studio album every two years. Nevertheless a barrage of events—a very public battle with Napster, James Hetfield's lengthy stint in rehab for painkiller addiction, and the unsurprising departure of Jason Newsted—put a full five years between *ReLoad* and *St. Anger*. Sober and sincere, Hetfield returned to the fold in late December 2001 to begin plotting the eighth studio album. Instead of hastily hiring a replacement for Newsted, the band recruited producer Bob Rock to play bass on the disc.

That wasn't the only change in the Metallica camp. To ensure Hetfield's continued sobriety, they hired psychotherapist and performance coach Phil Towle on the recommendation of Tom Morello after Towle refereed Audioslave's first tentative steps. With Metallica, Towle's prescription was a daily meeting at which band members aired their feelings and collaborated on songs.

"Our meetings give us an opportunity to connect with each other on a daily basis and to make sure that there wasn't anything in our personal lives that might come in and contaminate our professional lives," explained Kirk Hammett. "Talking . . . made a big difference and just opened up our communication, and gave us the confidence to go in and start writing lyrics based on whatever was going on in our lives. It just made the album much more personable."

"Personable" isn't the word that comes to mind upon hearing closing track "All Within My Hands," concerning a sexual power differential that finds Hetfield on the wrong side of the equation and ending with the chant *Kill! Kill! Kill!* He is stuck in the same frozen nightmare that inspired the self-inflicted malice of "Unforgiven," unable to move forward despite all that psychotherapy. Or perhaps expressing anger was part of the therapy. Regardless, Hetfield's sobriety dominates the album—it is the elephant in the room taking up the space where Hammett's guitar solos used to be.

As a consolation prize, Hammett got a hand in naming the disc. "The name *St. Anger* actually came from a St. Christopher medal I was wearing one day," he explained. "I was showing James that on the flip side it had a little surfer and the words 'Come back,' something a surfer is always concerned about. Out of nowhere he said, 'St. Anger!' I said, 'Wow, that's a great title' . . . When it became the time to write the lyrics, we all sat around and talked about how anger is both a positive thing and a negative thing, and the message of the song is that anger gets a bad rap. It's important for you to vocalize how you feel."

The title track is the album's psychic lynch pin, combining all the bombast and defiance of the band's earliest high-water marks, but with much more deliberate lyrics and an emotional nakedness not evident on earlier works. While not blazing any new territory, this high-velocity stomp through the time machine is exhilarating, returning Metallica to their uncomfortable comfort zone.

ST. ANGER

by Jaan Uhelszki

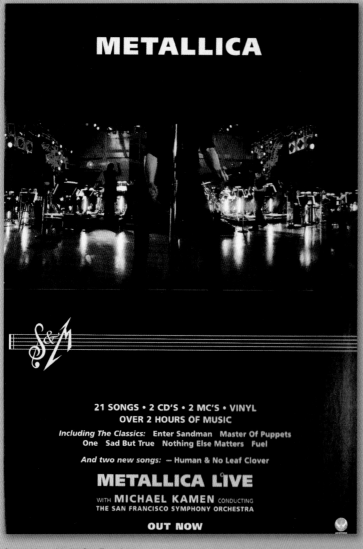

On working with the San Francisco Symphony, Newsted recalled—perhaps not surprisingly—that the biggest challenge was getting the relative volumes of the parties to sit well together. *All author collection*

"It's such a fucking blur," continues Urich, describing the making of the album at the time, but just as much describing the finished product itself. "We have a lot of material and in the last couple of days we're working on trying to nail it down. It's a new thing for us, because we had never done anything other than write. . . . We've never done the old, thirty songs and let's take the best ten. That's new for us. I think we were sort of guilty in the past, especially the *Load* and *ReLoad* stuff, of not editing ourselves. So we're dealing with that at the moment, which is kind of weird [laughs].

"Obviously it's been an interesting couple of years. I think there's some great energy. I don't know how to explain it. It's like it just bleeds differently. It's like if you peeled the skin off somebody and you know that layer . . . I think that [with] James' lyrics, and even some of the music, there's a kind of directness to it. It's about moments, or trying to not overthink it, overproduce it. We're trying not to beat the life out of it, which I think we had sort of done on the previous couple of records. It got to the point where we produced all the life out of it. So

there's some really great moments, some energy, some moments of people playing music together in a room, and it has a lot of soul. There's fast stuff, slow stuff, kind of super-heavy stuff, some stuff that's a little more experimental, fucked-up-sounding stuff. But I would say we're trying to hone it in and figure out, you know, what kind of statement do we want to make with this record?"

Whether it's a statement or not, *St. Anger* is certainly an oddball record. Wildly different than the previous three, differences range from Hetfield's emotionally raw singing to recurring nü-metal breakdowns and the near lack of anything akin to a guitar solo. But what got people talking most was nothing more than the sound of Ulrich's snare drum!

"When you make records you sort of divorce yourself from it afterwards," mused Ulrich. "I think it sounds awesome. When we were recording, we had two or three different drum kits in there and as we got a little further into the recording, we had the same drum kit setup that we recorded *Load* and *ReLoad* on. And it sounded really hi-fi. And one day I got kind of bored with it and I told

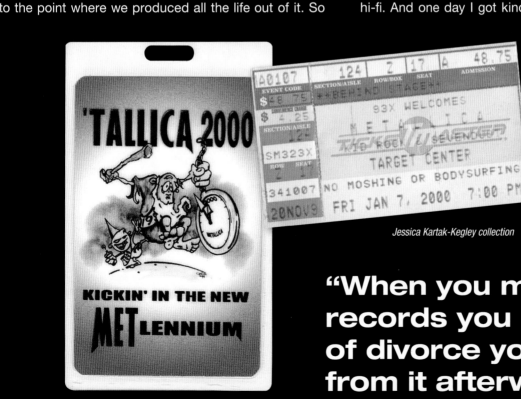

New millennium eve show, Pontiac Silverdome, Detroit, Michigan. *Author collection*

"When you make records you sort of divorce yourself from it afterwards."
—Lars Ulrich

my drum tech to set up different snare drums. I wanted him to kind of fuck with it every day, 'cause I didn't want to get too caught in the headspace of it. I wanted it as organic as possible. And then one day, the Rock set up a double bass kit in a different part of the room and instead of doing a bunch of close mic'ing, he did a bunch of ambient mic'ing. Like a couple of mics over the drum kit instead of close-mic'ing everything, and it was really cool and so garage-y and trashy. We sort of went with it from there. We stuck it out, which I was proud of, 'cause a lot of times in the past, when we'd done anything that was remotely out there, we had the tendency to always clean it up at the end. We really stuck with it and I'm super-proud of that. I think it sounds awesome.

"But it's also, to me, without getting too clichéd, it's like a moment in time. And this whole record, we try to define this record as a moment in time. It's like, 'Here is something that happened that day.' As we spent some time overdubbing and putting in the occasional guitar solo on there, it kept taking away from that moment in time. To me, and to all of us, this record was all about trying to capture a few moments because we felt a lot of the stuff that we had done the last couple of times

in the studio was not about that. It was about creating something, about executing something and we were just kind of sick of that. . . . And I'm proud to say we had the guts to see that through. It'll be interesting to see how it will age five years from now. After *. . . And Justice for All*, people started making records that sounded like that. Who knows? Let's see how it ages. I think it's kind of fun. It's always great to be part of something that shakes the foundations a little. I didn't really see this one coming. But I never see any of them coming. I just sit there in my own little ignorant world and do whatever is right for me and Metallica and then all of a sudden everybody has something to talk about afterwards."

"If it's not your cup of tea, it's not your cup of tea," continued Ulrich. "Certainly I can see that it's a challenging record. The main thing really was, after a while we started getting into the pummeling of it and initially when we were putting it together, I knew the songs were quite long. The songs were a little bit longer than I intended them to be initially when I was editing them. I was editing them a little longer 'cause I always edit longer and then I shorten as we go along. One element that started greatly appealing to us about what

All Author collection

"There's fast stuff, slow stuff, kind of super-heavy stuff, some stuff that's a little more experimental, f***ed-up-sounding stuff."

—Lars Ulrich

THE METALLIC-ERA

VOLUME II

MORE ORIGINAL TRACKS BY THE ORIGINAL ARTISTS AS COVERED BY METALLICA

Released in the U.K. in October 2001, The *Metallic-Era Vol. II* (like *Vol. I*, natch) collected original versions of songs by Diamond Head, Motörhead, Blue Öyster Cult, and others that Metallica had covered on the Garage releases. *Author collection*

Author collection

EChoBRain

New Album 4.17 in stores
[ECHOBRAIN]
Dylan Donkin (Vo.G.) Brian Sagrafena (Dr.) Jason Newsted (B.)
1. COLDER WORLD
2. THE FEELING IS OVER
3. SPOONFED
4. ADRIFT
5. KEEP ME ALIVE
6. GHOSTS
7. SUCKERPUNCH
8. HIGHWAY 44
9. I DRANK YOU
10. CRYIN' SHAME
11. ANJALI (Bonus Track for Japan Only)
+hidden track
SICP 118 ¥2,520 (w/t)

Side project Echobrain was Newsted's project with which to knock off raw EPs with well-regarded underground rockers at his own recording den, The Chophouse. *Author collection*

Much of *St. Anger* is forgotten and never played live, due partially to the band's admission that the songs were hugely stitched together and therefore difficult to reproduce. *Author collection*

METALLICA

[ST.ANGER]

JUNE.11th 2003 RELEASE

METALLICA / ST. ANGER
Frantic
St. Anger
Some Kind of Monster
Dirty Window
Invisible Kid
My World
Shoot Me Again
Sweet Amber
Unnamed Feeling
Purify
All Within My Hands

メタリカ「聖なる怒り」遂に解禁!!
朝代楽聞のニュー・アルバム「ST. ANGER」、6/11(水)いよいよその全貌が明らかに!!

驚きの内容とは!?

❶ 3面デジパック、DVD付き豪華2枚組セット!!
❷ しかもDVDの内容が何とアルバム収録曲全曲のスタジオ・ライヴ映像が収録!!
❸ 全世界永久仕様でのリリース!!

SICP 375-4 税込¥3,150 (w/t)

初回生産分のみ「メタリカ・オフィシャル・
グッズ・プレゼント応募ステッカー」付き!!

DOWNLOAD 2006
THE NEW SHOP is now... OPEN

Currently Online: 1

LINEUP STAGE TIMES NEWS TICKETS VIP TICKETS PARTNERS THE VILLAGE SNICKERS BOWL
SHOP FORUM INFO COMPETITION REGISTER DOWNLOAD.IE MOBILE GALLERY

DOWNLOAD

METALLICA LINKIN PARK
DONINGTON PARK
SATURDAY JUNE 5 & SUNDAY JUNE 6
CALL: 0870 5344 444 (24HRS)
DONINGTON PARK • DAY TICKETS: £45 / WEEKEND TICKETS: £80
WEEKEND + CAMPING: £90 / WEEKEND + LOADED CAMPING: £100
TICKETS: DOWNLOADFESTIVAL.CO.UK

CLEARCHANNEL ENTERTAINMENT KERRANG!

DOWNLOAD THE DOG

Download Festival, Donington, England, 2004.

FRIDAY 9 june	SATURDAY 10 june	SUNDAY 11 june
tool	**METALLICA**	**GN'R**
DEFTONES	KORN	FUNERAL FOR A FRIEND
COHEED & CAMBRIA	TRIVIUM	BULLET FOR MY
SOULFLY	AVENGED SEVENFOLD	VALENTINE
STRAPPING	STONE SOUR	CRADLE OF FILTH
YOUNG LAD	ALICE IN	LACUNA COIL
SOIL	CHAINS	IN FLAMES
WICKED WISDOM	ARCH ENEMY	36 CRAZYFISTS
AMPLIFIER	BLOOD SIMPLE	DRAGONFORCE
	SATYRICON	HATEBREED BREED 77

SNICKERS STAGE

the ALL-AMERICAN REJECTS	ALTER BRIDGE	the PRODIGY
ATREYU	OPETH	ALEXISONFIRE
INME	WITHIN TEMPTATION	EIGHTEEN VISIONS
CLUTCH	SECRET MACHINES	HUNDRED REASONS
FISHBONE	BILLY TALENT	AIDEN
DREDG	HENRY ROLLINS (SPOKENWORD)	FIGHTSTAR
BLEEDING THROUGH	DEVIL DRIVER	FROM FIRST TO LAST
GOJIRA	SIKTH	SOILWORK
THROWDOWN	JOHNNY TRUANT	ZEBRAHEAD
SUNS OF THE TUNDRA	KHOMA	GOD FORBID

Gibson PURE STAGE   myspace.com

GINGER & THE SONIC CIRCUS	KILLING JOKE	SICKOFITALL
BACKYARD BABIES	REUBEN	LORDI
CATHEDRAL	MONDO GENERATOR	SKINDRED
ENGERICA	LOUIE	MONEEN
BULLETS & OCTANE	THIS IS MENACE	DARKEST HOUR
MY AWESOME COMPILATION	10 YEARS	BLINDSIDE
ANIMAL ALPHA	FLYLEAF	MENDEED
the AUDITION	MANIC	BRING ME THE HORIZON
ENTER SHIKARI	IT DIES TODAY	the ZICO CHAIN
ART OF DYING	LIVING THINGS	VOODOO SIX
	EXIT TEN	LAUREN HARRIS
	:(	WINTERVILLE
	STONE GARD	STREETLIGHT YOUTH
		I-DEF-I

BOWL STAGE

GAY FOR JOHNNY DEPP	GET CAPE. WEAR CAPE. FLY.	VIKING SKULL
KEIKO	GET AMPED	BETTY CURSE
SINTUITION	THE HEDRONS	EVERGREY

STAGE TIMES NEWS TICKETS VIP TICKETS THE VILLAGE MOBILE GALLERY COMPETITIONS
FORUMS INFO REGISTER DOWNLOAD.IE PARTNERS 2005 SITE 2004 SITE SNICKERS BOWL   TOP▲

METALLICA
MADLY IN ANGER WITH THE WORLD TOUR
USA FALL 2004
PHOTO

Arrowhead Pond, Anaheim,
California, November 27, 2004.
Kevin Estrada collection.

Download Festival, Donington, England, 2004.

was going on was the pummeling effect of it, and the beating you were taking as you were listening to it. As we went to some of the junctures about, now let's make the song shorter, we decided to leave them long 'cause we thought there was a beauty in the pummeling effect. It was like, 'We could beat you up for five minutes, or we could beat you up for eight minutes. We'll beat you up for eight minutes instead. Put you through the ringer as much as possible.' And that was really where that came from. As we went along, we realized we were making a pretty challenging record, but it was so much fun."

Touring for *St. Anger*—the album debuted at No. 1 and has since gone double platinum—kicked off with a reprisal of the Summer Sanitarium idea, the band sharing stages with a bunch of nü-metal flashpoints, namely Mudvayne, Limp Bizkit, Linkin Park, and Deftones, with only the latter escaping widespread ridicule from the industry. November 2003 to November 2004 found the band on the more conventional Madly in Anger with the World tour, which was just that: a pan-world trip, plus a large North American campaign.

New to the Metalli-fold was bassist Robert Trujillo, who represented a connection to *St. Anger*–type metal via his work with Suicidal Tendencies. More recently he had been playing bass for Ozzy.

"Obviously they are very, very different," explained Ulrich, contrasting Trujillo and Newsted. "In a nutshell, Rob Trujillo is a little more of a traditional bass player in that he plays more with the drums. It's a little more rhythm section–oriented. Jason had a little more tendency to go with Hetfield, and go along more with the guitars obviously. Rob gives it a little more bottom 'cause he plays more with his fingers; a little more fullness. I feel a little more connected to him because of that. Jason had an incredible amount of energy, but it went more with the guitars. A lot of times it felt to me that there were three guitar players. People sit there and bitch that there is no bass on *. . . And Justice for All*. Well, try finding one place on the sixty-five minutes of the record where he's playing a different note. Either on the right hand picking differently, playing different notes, or the

www.WycoVintage.com

"Rob Trujillo is a little more of a traditional bass player in that he plays more with the drums."

—*Lars Ulrich*

Both Frank White collection

left hand. At some point it becomes like a third guitar. I'm not being disrespectful, dude; you're just asking me what the differences are.

"Mine and Rob's personality have a tendency to kind of gel a little more," added Ulrich. "I had a lot of respect for Jason, but sometimes our personalities . . . he was all about perfection and all this type of stuff. I'm a little more traditional rock 'n' roll, more about attitude, atmosphere, and vibe. We'd sit there and book five rehearsal dates and after two or three, me and James would be bored out of our minds. Jason would be going, 'We gotta practice more, practice more.'

"I would probably say out of any bass player I've ever played with, Rob probably is quickest to pick shit up effortlessly than anybody I've ever met. When we were doing the auditions back at HQ, we'd play three or four songs and I'd go, 'Is there anything else you want to play?' And somebody said 'Sad but True,' and he didn't know it.

And in ten minutes we went through it perfectly. That kind of thing. He has a rather effortless relationship to the bass guitar. Like for instance the first Fillmore show, we sat down and wrote a set list that afternoon and I had changed the set list like thirty minutes before the show and I didn't want to play anything like really obvious. So I looked at the back catalog and I said, 'What about "Phantom Lord?"' Rob goes, 'I've never heard that song.' And it's like thirty minutes before show time. He threw the CD Walkman on and listened to 'Phantom Lord' twice. We ran through it two or three times and an hour later we played 'Phantom Lord.' Not necessarily the version to end all versions, but at least he fuckin' played it. . . . And that kind of spirit is really important for where this band is at right now. We've been changing the set list around, playing different songs and trying to fuck it up and not get stuck in a rut of the same set list and the same Hetfield raps. Rob just really fits that vibe quite well."

Designer: Randy Tuten/www.rtuten.com

SUNDAY, JULY 16th
SUMMER SANITARIUM TOUR
METALLICA
KORN · KID ROCK
POWERMAN 5000 · SYSTEM OF A DOWN
LIVE AT THE
SCHNEPF FARMS FESTIVAL SITE
N CREEK, AZ

Designer: Lindsey Kuhn/www.swampco.com

Jessica Kartak-Kegley collection

Frank White collection

9.
DEATH OR GLORY
2008–2010

"I don't think we're content being down here. There are some bands who are fine with it. They love what they do and they don't like change—they're afraid of it. That's fine. We got somethin' up our asses that makes us want to go, 'We've done that, let's do something else, I'm bored, let's go somewhere.' We've had that hunger since day one. That, mixed with total, pure, from the heart honesty."
—James Hetfield, *Brave Words & Bloody Knuckles*, 2003

Embattled after *St. Anger* and its not-so-heavy touring cycle, the Metallica guys settled even further into lives outside the band, taking much of 2005 off. One spot of fun was opening for the Rolling Stones in San Francisco's AT&T Park in November. In 2006, they issued a DVD called *The Videos 1989–2004*, one of the best-received and useful visual packages from the band since the beloved commemorative *Cliff 'Em All* back in 1987.

Sane and healthy. August 2008. *Joby Sessions*/Total Guitar *Magazine via Getty Images*

The following year was spent back on the job, writing for a new record and touring, the band mounting a campaign called Escape from the Studio '06 (follow-up to Escape from the Studio '95) on which they road-tested a few bits of new material and, on occasion, played *Master of Puppets* in its entirety, commemorating the twentieth anniversary of that classic.

Eventually, there it was, *Death Magnetic*, Metallica's ninth studio album, and for the first time in four records, Bob Rock was not producing, replaced by the controversial Rick Rubin, who gave Metallica a sound somewhere between his second effort for Trouble, *Manic Frustration*, and his only for Wolfsbane, *Live Fast, Die Fast*. What the band was really looking for was the Rick Rubin philosophy (when he was around to give it).

"What really attracted us was [Rubin's] ability to get the essence of the band, to strip away," Hetfield told me in a tuning room while on tour for the record. "Obviously, there's a lot of bands that he's done that we liked. And when we hear the record, it's pretty stripped down. Obviously the Johnny Cash stuff: his voice, and a guitar [laughs]— that's really all he needs. He was able to strip him back down to that. Stuff like the Cult, you know, stuff that used to be big and '80s-sounding, he stripped it down to where what you can really hear is the band, and the best parts of the band. That's what we wanted from him."

As for the spirit of the album, "it certainly is a lot of embracing of our past, and it's well known in the press that Rick Rubin got us focusing on *Master of Puppets* and the early

Frank White collection

Silverlake Conservatory of Music Benefit, Wiltern Theatre, Los Angeles, May 14, 2008.
Kevin Winter/Getty Images

Kevin Estrada collection

KROQ Weenie Roast Y Fiesta, Verizon Wireless Amphitheater, Irvine, California, May 17, 2008. *Noel Vasquez/Getty Images*

This spread: Sprint Center, Kansas City, Missouri, October 25, 2008. *Both © ZUMA Wire Service/Alamy*

days," Hetfield went on. "You know, 'Let's go back in time there, and feel what you were feeling then' and all of this, and unlearn a lot of life, which is impossible. But we understood the feeling he wanted, that hunger and that drive of the early albums. It was pretty easy to go there, surprisingly, once we all started feeling it again. And it's one of those things that, if you think too much about writing a certain way, it's not going to work. You can't. You've just got to be there and you've got to feel it, and it just so happened that it felt right when we were doing it."

As for the present, Hetfield offered, "As far as listening to new bands, there are so many unbelievable musicians out there that are over the top, as far as their talent, and it's pretty inspiring. I pick up a guitar and I look at YouTube, and whoever is on there doing some guitar lessons, like say the Dragonforce or Trivium guys, and they're just going [makes shredding sounds]. 'Okay, again. Okay, now do it faster.' Are you kidding me?! It's unbelievable. Unbelievable! 'And here it is backwards, and here it is with one hand.' And drummers, too. I mean, the drummers are like . . . they're lead guitar players on their kicks. It's just unbelievable. So that's pretty inspiring. So obviously we're not chasing anything. I'm not chasing the best singer award or best rhythm player. We are what we are, and we're as good as we are [laughs]. But together we create some kind of magic that maybe some other bands can't, so that's the part we like to focus on."

As Hetfield put more and more distance between himself and rehab, he was able to reduce his need for so much structure, as seen throughout the *Some Kind of Monster* documentary. "Now he'll be like, 'Hey, let's go check out Social Distortion or see the Police,'" Trujillo said. "He's more into hanging out now. It's like he's got his juju back. Back then, I just remember him being a bit more fragile. You've also got to understand, he was really reconnecting with his personal life, in terms of his family, and reexisting, not just in the band, but with his daily lifestyle. And it seems like now, here we have *Death Magnetic*, and it's not like, 'OK, it's four o'clock, I've got to leave this minute.' Puts down the guitar and he's done.

Newsted and Trujillo double the bottom end at the 24th Annual Rock and Roll Hall of Fame induction ceremony, Public Hall, Cleveland, Ohio, April 4, 2009. *Theo Wargo/WireImage/Getty Images*

Frank White collection

Or working on a cool guitar part, 'Oh, shoot, it's eleven. I've gotta go.' Now it's like, we're working on something cool, and there's not really a time constraint on his creativity anymore . . . I mean, he's absolutely committed and involved with *Death Magnetic*, and beyond. This has become a labor of love for him."

The end result is a record stuffed with superlative riffs, usually many in succession, making for long songs. The most direct comparison, obviously, is *Justice*, with the main difference being *Death*'s white-hot production (some say compressed to the point of error), and the fact that most of the parts are much catchier, though almost never slow, in contrast to the catchy-groove yardstick that was *Metallica*.

"For one thing, Rick has always got the best team around him," Trujillo said when asked about Rubin's role in bringing Metallica to the stylistic sweet spot that defines *Death Magnetic*. "He's got the best engineers, I feel. Greg Fidelman was amazing. He knew the songs as well or better than us. And I thought that was a major factor. He worked his ass off on this. . . . But I also feel that Rick is a great song doctor. Rick is a man of great words and suggestions. . . . James is a great singer. He's still got a strong voice, he can still hit the upper register pretty well, and Rick was instrumental in reuniting James with that dynamic. And I don't know that if we worked with somebody else, producing this, that would've happened. And that sent chills down my spine, in a good way. It was so exciting to hear James singing and be a natural A440, and singing in a higher register. To me, there's more angst. It's not so safe. And Rick was instrumental in that. And reuniting Lars and James with the style of arranging from the earlier years, which is something that I feel that those two were maybe even trying to run away from for so many years. It was almost like the older material, it seemed like it was almost joked about at times. The guys would play edited versions of stuff from *Master of Puppets* and, you know, I think that it's great that they reunited with the idea of the past and celebrated it. Not to say that *Death Magnetic* sounds exactly like any of those albums, but

Prudential Center, Newark, New Jersey, February 1, 2009.
Kevin Hodapp photo/Frank White Photo Agency

just in terms of arranging and riffs and conceptually, I think there is an element to that."

Death Magnetic is most definitely a complicated, heavy album. "The Judas Kiss," "All Nightmare Long," and "That Was Just Your Life" move from strength to strength, packed with innovative twists and turns, memorable verses, breaks, prechoruses, and choruses. Yet despite their lengths, they never get oppressive. Prerelease single "Cyanide" is effortlessly headbanging and "The Day That Never Comes" just might be the band's most successful semi–power ballad, with a classy and poignant video to boot. And throughout, Ulrich is back thrashing away, lacing in his uniquely spare yet rhythmically complex fills, spurred on by the quick right hand of Hetfield, who roils up thrashing storms, but with wind speeds slightly reduced, to create pockets of energy. One of the most enigmatic tracks is also the record's shortest, "My Apocalypse," being obtuse of melody, "comfortably" thrashy, and indicative of a band with a sixth sense for this.

"Actually, we would butt heads about it, in some way, in the reverse," said Ulrich, when asked if Rubin had pushed for shorter songs and fewer riffs. "Everything we did creatively with the songs was done in preproduction. Rick didn't want us to go anywhere near the recording studio until the songs were one hundred percent done. And so we're sitting in preproduction, and he was like, 'Let's make that ending longer.' And me and James would kind of look at each other. 'Play the ending twice as long, huh?! Okay.' . . . So there was never anything about the long songs whatsoever. . . . I think what Rick does is that it's not about long songs, short songs, any of that.

"I mean, obviously most of these Johnny Cash songs are two minutes long and [the Red Hot] Chili Peppers or whatever. To him it's about the epitome of what each band is. And he was the one that spent a long time talking about, how can I say this, making us comfortable about going back to that style of Metallica again. We've been tentative about that for about eighteen years [laughs]. . . . But with this stuff, Rick was the one who encouraged us to go longer and to think more like the eighties and to not be afraid of being inspired by most records from the eighties and that whole thing. There was definitely nothing about any of his stuff that was about shortening anything."

And as for the enigmatic "death magnetic" concept, "the lyrics are open to interpretation," said Trujillo. "That's one of the brilliant things I feel with Hetfield and Metallica. My take and interpretation of 'death magnetic' is, you know, death is a polarity. Death is constantly kind of there. Of course it's there and it is sucking every one of us in. But how you deal with it is a whole 'nother thing. Like riding out a hundred-foot wave in surfing or something— that to me is death magnetic. It is riding that fine line, that edge, that tightrope between being gone into existing on a higher plane. And you can also relate that to rock 'n' roll. A lot of our fallen heroes, people like Layne Staley, rode the same edge but in terms of being euphoric and being high and then having it consume them, unfortunately. That's the unfortunate side. That is my view on the title *Death Magnetic*—the polarity of death, and how it can draw you in, and how people handle it."

Said Ulrich with respect to the odd title and phrase, "We sat down, the boys in the band, and Peter [Mensch] and Cliff [Burnstein], and it was one of those, 'Okay boys, stop fucking around, let's come up with an album title.

Toronto, October 26, 2009. *Author collection*

Prudential Center, Newark, New Jersey, January 31, 2009. *Frank White collection*

September 2009. *Steve Brown/ Photoshot/Getty Images*

AT&T Center, San Antonio, Texas, September 28, 2009. Jay West/WireImage/Getty Images

By 2008 Metallica had some catching up to do—with its own past. Years of constant reinvention and pushing the musical envelope almost beyond recognition had left the band distanced from hardcore metal fans, not least the newest generation that now worshipped at the altar of new musical blood-letters like Trivium and Lamb of God. So when it was announced Rick Rubin would produce the next Metallica album, the long-suffering faithful cheered. Rubin was the man who had signed Slayer and produced *Reign in Blood*, still regarded as the greatest thrash metal album of all.

"He's all about the big picture," said Lars Ulrich. "Rick's a vibe guy." The producer came in with one piece of advice: "Imagine you're not Metallica," Rubin told them. "You don't have any hits to play and you have to come up with material to play in a battle of the bands. What do you sound like?" This was the sort of statement, James Hetfield explained, that gave the project instant focus.

The result was the most thrash-conscious Metallica album since *Master of Puppets* more than two decades prior. From the ponderous sound of the heartbeat that opens the album (as if the broken body of Metallica was coming slowly back to life) to front cover image of a coffin (a motif that would feature throughout the two-year world tour that followed) to the album's title (an oblique reference to how so many rock stars have died young, as if magnets for death), *Death Magnetic* was Metallica going back to its twisted roots, and doing so in style.

All but one of the ten tracks are over six minutes long, and all are credited equally to the four members, something that had decidedly *not* happened back in the '80s. The cowriting is underscored by brainstorming tracks like "That Was Just Your Life" and "The End of the Line." Where even the Black Album would then have gone for contrast, *Death* simply got harder, faster, with bones-into-dust muthas like "Broken, Beat & Scarred" and, most head-splattering of all, the truly epic "All Nightmare Long."

Significantly, none of the tracks fade out, either. They simply vanish into flames. The other standout moment is "The Unforgiven III," a moving piano soliloquy, with strings and horns extemporizing over the atmospheric intro of the original before moving into a song nearly eight minutes long, like "Nothing Else Matters" meets "Orion." It's the only self-consciously slow track on an album determined to complete the circle, including the most enormous guitar-fest three-quarters of the way through—a real love it or hate it moment, and better for it.

After that, however, is where the album really takes off, beginning with "The Judas Kiss," eight more minutes recalling the band that recorded "Sad but True" *and* "Disposable Heroes," with more frantic-by-the-moment Kirk Hammett soloing that painstakingly puts Humpty Dumpty back together again only to create a sound that is more than just the '80s revisited. This is the sound of the future.

This feeling reaches its apotheosis on the nearly ten-minute instrumental "Suicide & Redemption," a big "Call of Ktulu" moment that, against the odds, blows up into one of the album's highlights.

Suddenly, it was like *Load* never happened. Like *St. Anger* had been some sort of fucked-up joke. Suddenly, almost without trying, it seemed, Metallica was once again the fiercest, most fulsome and fiery heavy metal band in the world. Bar none. And for once everyone agreed. *Death Magnetic* became a colossal success, going straight to No. 1 in thirty-two countries—the first time that had happened since *Load* twelve years before—proving that metal fans would take primetime, thrash-era Metallica over postmodern, Napster-baiting, therapist-consulting Metallica any day of the headbanging week.

DEATH MAGNETIC

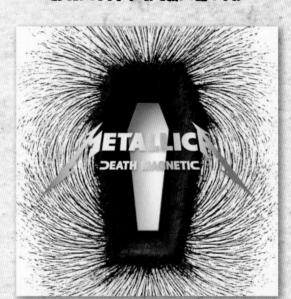

by Mick Wall

Sonisphere Festival, Warsaw, June 16, 2010.
Kevin Nixon/Metal Hammer Magazine via Getty Images

Frank White collection

And we sat there and threw a bunch of different things around for the better part of the day. And Kirk Hammett, one of the lyrics in the song 'My Apocalypse' has the words 'death magnetic' in it, and we were sitting there looking at this option and that option and whatever, and *Death Magnetic* came up as an option. Initially we were all a little 'Huh?,' but as the day wore on there was an abstract element in it that was pretty cool. I was really pushing for the title *Suicide and Redemption*, because that was something we were kicking around for a year or two, and I felt that that really covered a lot of the lyrical elements of the record. But the idea of having the word *suicide* in an album title [laughs], let's not make it so fucking depressing right out of the box that people are going to be tuned out even before they hear it. So *Death Magnetic* came up, and it had kind of a really poetic beautiful abstract vibe to it, and we ended up kicking that around and picking it.

"I was blown away how awesome they were, and how poetic they were, and how very different they were than I expected," Ulrich further noted when asked about Hetfield's writing, equally as introspective as his work on *St. Anger* but somehow less fragile and self-pitying, more bold and affirmative. "Because when we last talked about it, I'm still expecting more kind of storytelling, more stuff with a dramatic arc to it and so on. And then came all this almost poetry-like stuff that blew my mind. I saw how beautiful it was. But I was really, on the second front, surprised about how dark and fucked up it was, and I was almost, as a friend, a little scared and kind of surprised about how much dark energy and sort of unresolved dark stuff is still going on in his mind [laughs]. It kind of threw me. Because I'm forty-four, James is close to that, maybe forty-five, we live here, the sun shines

Designer: Print Mafia/www.printmafia.net

every day. It's like, we take care of our kids, show up at HQ, and we blast out this pretty nutty heavy metal stuff, but I mean, we're not by nature super-dark fucked-up people. We're happy-go-lucky dudes like everyone else in their forties. And I was pretty stunned when he showed that side of it. . . .

"They are abstract, they are poetic, and me and Rick were talking about it, there was this word that Rick came up with: 'gutspill.' There are these momentary thoughts of just gutspill, kind of write down what goes on in your mind at any given moment. And I was pretty fucking

Designer: Dave Hunter/www.gammalyte.com

ago [laughs]. Last time it was a completely democratic process. We sat there with pen and paper. But this time around, I started off by trying to see if there was some stuff that we could do together. And I realized very early on that this was something he had to go through himself. So I left him alone. . . ."

Asked whether Hetfield "owned" those lyrics or whether they reflected a state of mind that had hopefully passed, Ulrich mused, "He generally doesn't want to talk a lot about it. I don't want to tap on the door or knock on the door—you don't get very far. I can tell you, I've read him talk about a lot of it, and a lot of other guys and Layne Staley and this and that, all these other peers of his, and obviously there is a lot more of him in there than he feels comfortable acknowledging. I think that's pretty evident. And I think the way that stuff comes out, it's easier for him to third person it. Put it on somebody else. Use other people as another way to extract that out of himself. I think that's totally cool, but I think a lot of that stuff is obviously about himself. And that's what makes it so difficult. Because on a day-to-day basis, you kind of sit there and go, 'Holy fuck, that's a lot to carry around!' [laughs]. And you don't want your best friend to carry that around. You kind of hope that it's all cool in there."

Hetfield's emotional well-being aside, *Death Magnetic* was almost universally well-received, racking up double-platinum status in the United States for sales of over two million copies, likely the last big gasp for a heavy metal record in terms of physical sales as the world began transitioning to digital. As well, the record debuted at No. 1, making Metallica the first band to hit the top spot with five consecutive studio albums. Touring for the record found the band relaxed, often playing in the round, hitting most corners of the world with a bevy of highly respected pure-metal bands in tow. Backup acts such as Lamb of God, Mastodon, Machine Head, Orphaned Land, Fear Factory, Sepultura Down, and the Sword served notice that Metallica was going to fight to keep their metal turf—and no one doubted their odds, given the massive headbang they'd just received through the thrash magic of *Death Magnetic*.

stunned that so much shit still existed inside his mind. But once I wrapped my head around them and kind of weaned myself from what I was expecting, it really works for me. So I'm super proud of them. And it was also a little . . . this is the most he's been alone. Because back in the day we did a lot of it together. We would watch movies together, read books together, talk about topics and ideas and stuff like that, and all of this is obviously well documented. There's a movie there a couple years

NASHVILLE
09·14·09

METALLICA

SOMMET CENTER

PRESENTED BY FRANK PRODUCTIONS AND OUTBACK CONCERTS

SK Olimpiisky. Moscow, April 24, 2010. © ZUMA Wire Service/Alamy

AC1026   119   11 18   COMP   EAC1026
  0.00 ALL GATE ACCESS   0.00   13:10
                   WWW.LIVENATION.COM   CN 07640
119   METALLICA   119
TM   19X   WWW.METALLICA.COM   TMMLA404
 11 18   AIR CANADA CENTRE   11
ILA404C   GST #126007780   0.00
260CT09   MON OCT 26 2009 7:00PM
05444404677

M1029   114   G   2 $86.00   M1029
EVENT CODE SECTION/AISLE ROW/BOX SEAT ADMISSION
                                          PRICE $86.00
                                          +CRF: $2.30
       11.15   GST: $3.84
SECTION/AISLE   WWW.LIVENATION.COM   PST: $7.68
                   METALLICA
                   WWW.METALLICA.COM   114
ROW   SEAT   GST #R126007780   114
 11   G
                   TUES NOV 3, 2009 7:00PM
                   SCOTIABANK PLACE
  G   2   2
77739771914439
METALLICA WORLD MAGNETIC TOUR

"But when I go back and listen to *Death Magnetic*, I go, 'Oh wow, oh, that's the lyrics, or the riff's like that?!' It's already morphed into something else, you know?"
—James Hetfield

"They're super-comfy on stage," Hetfield said of the new album's many regularly played songs, namely "That Was Just Your Life," "The End of the Line," "Broken, Beat & Scarred," "Cyanide," and "The Day That Never Comes." "That's a good sign, because when you're writing something that you have to sit and really think about, or you're constructing something in the studio . . . you know, a lot of . . . *And Justice for All* and even *Puppets* was two or three songs shoved into one. But these just float a lot better. They came out a lot easier, and that's always a good sign. When you're playing them, they're easy to remember [laughs]. But they do feel good on stage; they feel great, actually. And it's interesting, we probably played more songs from this, maybe not since the Black Album. On the Black Album we ended up playing a lot of new songs too. And I haven't really gone back and listened to the record. It's like we're still breaking the songs in. But when I go back and listen to *Death Magnetic*, I go, 'Oh wow, oh, that's the lyrics, or the riff's like that?!' It's already morphed into something else, you know? But that's a pretty natural thing.

"It's really geared towards us remaining sane and healthy," Hetfield continued, commenting on touring. "We have a voodoo doctor out with us, which is very important, for the road. I just call him that because he does everything [laughs]. From making us special drinks [holds up a drink] to chiropractic, massage, and acupuncture, putting needles in us! Just taking care of ourselves much better as far as our health goes, eating a lot better. Obviously the partying, in my area, has toned down quite a bit [laughs]. And summertime, having the families out as much as possible. It's just a healthier lifestyle in general, out on the road. Seeing some of these bands that are out with us, some are still partying super hard and you look at that and go, 'Wow, that was us. Okay, that's your path, go for it, you got it.' And then other bands are, 'Well, tell me a little more about this or that.' They're a lot more health-conscious. It's no longer uncool to say, 'No, I'm not having a beer right now. I want to stay focused.' Or, 'I'm going to work out tomorrow morning.' It's okay to take care of yourself."

Frank White collection

10.
SECRETS IN MY HEAD
2011–2015

"They are my metal blood brothers. They're very brave, and they can play. I'm not easy to play with. Some of [*Lulu*] that sounds easy is actually really hard. A lot of cool players can't do that. Academia drove it out of them."
—Lou Reed, *USA Today*, 2011

The riff-mad heavy metal triumph that is *Death Magnetic* seemed such a sweet way to end this tale. But Metallica doesn't settle, ever, and they would soon gleefully jump into the bad books of metal fans once again with an incendiary collaboration to blow up the rock world.

But first, on January 14, 2009, Metallica received their Rock and Roll Hall of Fame induction notice and were formally welcomed in by Flea from the Red Hot Chili Peppers on April 24. Cliff Burton's father Ray accepted on behalf of his fallen son, and both Robert Trujillo and Jason Newsted performed with the band. Further recognizing their roots, in 2010 and 2011, the band performed a number of high-profile shows as part

Sorting anger, using it positively. Palace Grounds, Bangalore, India, October 30, 2011. © *epa european pressphoto agency b.v./Alamy*

of thrash's original "Big Four" with Slayer, Anthrax, and Megadeth. Ulrich and Dave Mustaine finally buried the hatchet, even though Mustaine had declined an invitation to the Hall of Fame induction.

The incendiary collaboration previously referenced was, of course, with Lou Reed, the odd couple building a full record of original material. *Lulu*, issued on Halloween 2011, featured a mountain of variously harsh, profane, and inscrutable Reed poetry (shaped by a narrative based on two plays by Frank Wedekind), mostly spoken over surging, jammy Metallica riffs 'n' rhythms recorded, unsurprisingly, with a deft combination of power and brightness.

Hetfield told Argentina's Rock & Pop 95.9FM that the Reed collaboration germinated at the Rock and Roll Hall of Fame induction ceremony. "We jammed with him on the twenty-fifth-year anniversary, and after the playing, he felt so good, he felt so alive that backstage there were some friends of his coming up to us and saying, 'What did you do to him? We've never seen him smile so much.' And then he just yelled down the hallway as we were leaving, 'We should do a record together.' And we thought, 'Yeah, right. Is he talking to us?' [laughs]. But he was serious. He had told us that we're the band he always wanted to have. And I agreed—Metallica is the band I always wanted to have as well [laughs]."

"It's definitely different," continued Hetfield. "This is not the new Metallica studio record. This is *Lulu*. And that's why we named it *Lulu*—it's not Metallica, it's not Lou Reed. It's us together making something called *Lulu*. I'm sure there's some Metallica fans that will think that 'This

"An Evening with Lou Reed and Metallica," Cologne, Germany, November 11, 2011.
Peter Wafzig/Getty Images

Sonisphere Festival, Warsaw, May 10, 2012.

Mustaine (as well as Jason Newsted and even Ron McGovney) joined the band for the thirtieth-anniversary shows at The Fillmore in San Francisco, December 7 and 10, 2011. *Tim Mosenfelder/WireImage/Getty Images*

Download Festival, Donington, England, 2012.

In October 2009 Metallica joined Lou Reed at the Rock and Roll Hall of Fame's twenty-fifth anniversary concert at Madison Square Garden for versions of the Velvet Underground's "Sweet Jane" and "White Light/White Heat." The performance was fun enough (and not quite the trainwreck audience members had anticipated) for Reed to suggest the two musical powerhouses collaborate on an album in the near future. That album, *Lulu* (released on Halloween 2011), turned out to be a ninety-five-minute shockwave to Metallica fans, observers, and—let's be honest here—*general logic*. The fact that *Lulu* is the most reviled (critically and among a ruling majority of fans) title in a discography that's had its fair share of creatively alienating statements is such a part of the album's legacy that it bears mentioning before examining the collection of songs with the most objectivity the actual results will allow.

Essentially, *Lulu* is Lou Reed's baby, thanks to his governing concept for the album: Lyrics based on German playwright Frank Wedekind's two "Lulu" plays, *Erdgeist* (*Earth Spirit*, 1895) and *Die Büchse der Pandora* (*Pandora's Box*, 1904). James Hetfield's vocal contributions are few—Metallica is Reed's backing band, as evidenced by their billing. Nonetheless, Hetfield became the unwitting proprietor of a viral meme thanks to his howled proclamation of *I Am the Table!!!* toward the end of prerelease track (and album opener) "The View." Reed's lyrics are largely sexually depraved in nature (the Lulu character is a prostitute), keeping with the source material, but updated with abstract and, again, unwitting absurdity. On top of this, the delivery usually finds itself at the most tuneless end of his range. That's saying a lot, given Reed's body of work.

Barring "The View," *Lulu* primarily comprises eight-minute-plus tracks. Metallica's role here is not a huge departure from the chunky hugeness they have been perfecting, on and

by Andrew Earles

off, since 1991's Black Album, but the results sound more like outtakes than any progression of the style. Add to that the nature of Reed's vocal half of the equation and it's hard to escape the idea that the whole album sounds like the two parties were nowhere near one another during the recording.

Regarded collectively, Metallica's first three albums—*Kill 'Em All* (1983), *Ride the Lightning* (1984), and *Master of Puppets* (1985)—show an arc of heavy metal development, impact, and upper-echelon quality equaled only by Black Sabbath's invention of the genre itself almost fifteen years earlier, a context that must be considered in the wake of *Lulu*, even if the latter resides in a separate solar system from the aforementioned classics. And that is because, regardless of genre, cultural tenure, long-term success, or massive and rabid fan base, if *Lulu* had come from any other band, it would have been total career suicide. Additionally, Metallica has a mechanism in place, creatively and publicity-wise, that allows them to fully recover from their missteps. Part of that mechanism is wholly intangible but could be their most important driving factor: Metallica carries the endearing habit of making its mistakes in public—whether those mistakes are albums, images changes, or legal stances—and owning them like real people own mundane choices that might lead to regret. For every *Ride the Lightning* or *Master of Puppets*, there's a Napster, a *Lulu*, a money-devouring psychiatrist, or a vexing application of eyeliner.

There's one thing that all of this proves, something that critics don't want to dwell upon because it makes for content that our failure-obsessed, reality-addicted culture can't wrap its collective head around: that Metallica is the world's first mega-band to be . . . mega-human. And *Lulu* is the best proof yet.

s the new Metallica record. I don't like it. I'm scared.' And t's not. This is a project that was presented to us that we wanted to challenge ourselves with. I mean, there's some great riffs on there. There's not a lot of singing from me on it. It's Lou and his lyrics, with us writing background music for Lou. So that's what we did. There will be fans that it will be difficult for them to understand, but we can't stop being Metallica, we can't stop exploring what we wanna do as an artist. We don't like limiting ourselves. But we're not doing it just to mess with the fans; that's for sure. If they don't like it, wait until the next record where we're fully focused on Metallica, which we're actually writing right now.

"We would love to do some shows—I don't know how many, I don't know where. How many can we do together? t doesn't need to be twenty shows and it doesn't need to be one show—somewhere in the middle there, I think, o give everyone a taste of it and just see what it's like.

It's an intense record and Lou has stated that he doesn't know if he can do the whole thing. But I think he will and I think he certainly can. It's a very unique concept—it's not a Metallica concert; it's not anthem rock whatsoever. This is kind of lonely . . . it's like one-person music, in a way, for me. I don't need to listen to it with other people; it distracts me, actually. I like listening to it by myself. So it will be probably small, dark places [laughs]. Like my mind [laughs]."

The *Lulu* live situation never happened, whether due to the project's ill reception or not. Instead, Metallica sat coiled and ready to follow up the fantastic *Death Magnetic* with a record they promised to be on par with those sparks-a-flyin' songs, and again with Rick Rubin at the production helm.

To underscore the band's ability to write volumes in this dastardly direction, in January 2012 Metallica issued *Beyond Magnetic*, which featured four additional songs

from the *Death Magnetic* sessions. The slamming nature of these songs proved that the creative well was full up and ready to be tapped.

As for Hetfield—the soul and beating heart of Metallica—he says that he still has anger in him, but he's finally sorted out how to use it positively. "It's fueled my life. Along with other things that fuel my life now as well. But you know, we've all got our thing. We've all got our defect, of sorts, that we've hung onto, that seemed to work for us, or we're wanting to shake or work on—there's still some there. As far as anger goes, it's not just anger anymore, for sure. I get to display it in my work. Lars, his defects come out other places [laughs], where people aren't reading them, I would guess. But we all have our stuff that we work on. I'm able to express it. That's one of the easiest things for me to express, so that's kind of where and how it goes."

The enthusiastic embrace of *Death Magnetic* by long-discerning Metallica fans has helped bring positivity to the band as well. "Amazing. Very, very surreal still,"

Nova Rock 2012, Nickelsdorf, Austria, June 10, 2012. © epa european pressphoto agency b.v./Alamy

Designer: Nate Duval/www.nateduval.com

Designer: David Caron/www.hoverchairstudios.com

Horsens State Prison, Horsens, Denmark,
June 6, 2012. © epa european
pressphoto agency b.v./Alamy

Outside Lands Music and Arts Festival,
San Francisco, August 11, 2012.
Jeff Kravitz/FilmMagic/Getty Images

muses Hetfield. "Thinking that, you know, we were just about to break up or yell each other into not wanting to be with each other anymore and then we come out stronger than ever and put together an album that feels like we're alive again. . . . And obviously, getting some positive response back, it helps, man. No matter what—I don't want to speak for all artists—but at the end of the day the artist says, 'We're doing this for us; I'm doing this for me,' but yes, it feels good when someone else says you did a great job. It's human."

Despite the conspicuous absence of a new studio record from the band in the seven years since *Death Magnetic*, the band has been busy confounding the industry and, well, just having fun—but, admirably, not alone; instead, with their fans.

In the summers of 2012 and 2013, the band executed their own Orion Music + More festival gigs. June 23 and 24, 2012, found the band and a ragtag army of entertainers in Atlantic City, New Jersey, where thirty-seven acts were slated to play, with the headliners performing all of *Ride the Lightning* on the Saturday and all of *Metallica* on the Sunday. June 8 and 9 of the following year, the organization took the show to Detroit, where a similar mix of punk, myriad metal styles, and even rave-type music competed for fans' attentions, along with a car and motorcycle show; a Metallica museum;

Just a sampling of Metallica tribute CDs down through the years.

Voodoo Experience, New Orleans, Louisiana, October 27, 2012. *Chelsea Lauren/WireImage/Getty Images*

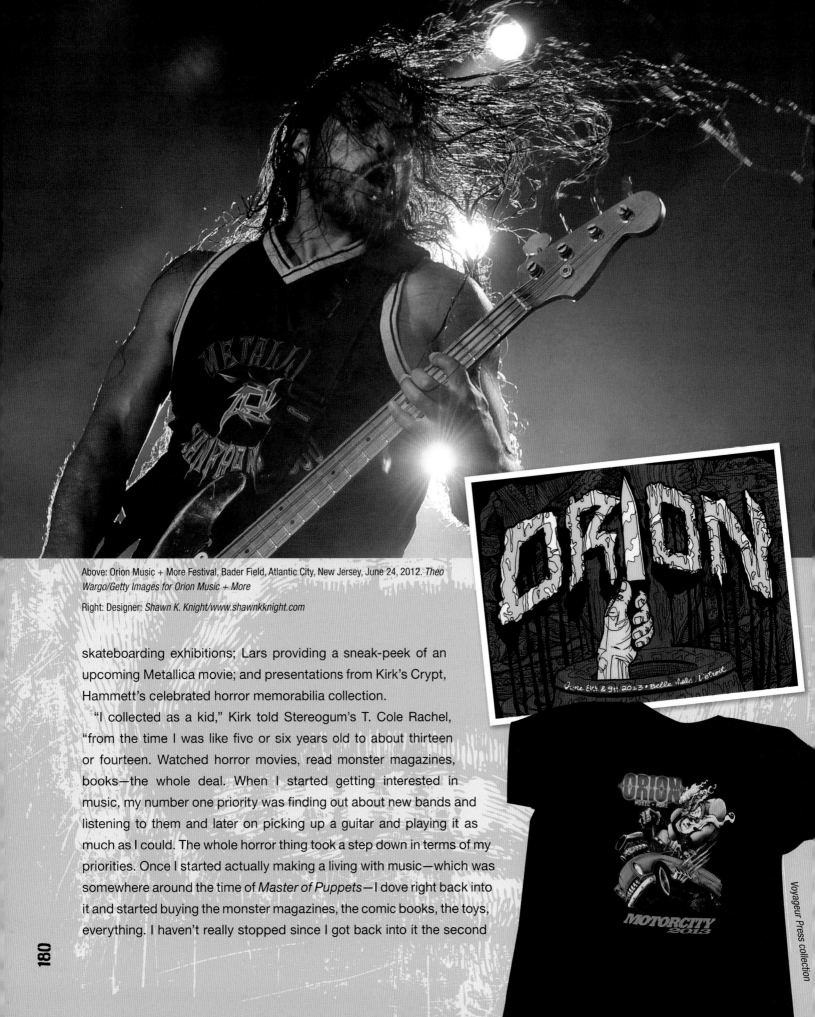

Above: Orion Music + More Festival, Bader Field, Atlantic City, New Jersey, June 24, 2012. *Theo Wargo/Getty Images for Orion Music + More*

Right: Designer: *Shawn K. Knight/www.shawnkknight.com*

skateboarding exhibitions; Lars providing a sneak-peek of an upcoming Metallica movie; and presentations from Kirk's Crypt, Hammett's celebrated horror memorabilia collection.

"I collected as a kid," Kirk told Stereogum's T. Cole Rachel, "from the time I was like five or six years old to about thirteen or fourteen. Watched horror movies, read monster magazines, books—the whole deal. When I started getting interested in music, my number one priority was finding out about new bands and listening to them and later on picking up a guitar and playing it as much as I could. The whole horror thing took a step down in terms of my priorities. Once I started actually making a living with music—which was somewhere around the time of *Master of Puppets*—I dove right back into it and started buying the monster magazines, the comic books, the toys, everything. I haven't really stopped since I got back into it the second time, which was around 1985. There were two aspects to my collecting: when I collected as a kid—and sadly I don't have anything from back then, though I wish I did—and then when I got back into it. What you see in my book, *Too Much Horror Business*, and on *Toy Hunter* is the latter part of my collecting. I got into the stuff and I never really got out of it. Its allure never really faded with me. I love the stuff as much as I've ever loved it; sometimes I think I love it more. I definitely don't love it less."

On the record front, November 2012 saw Metallica's departure from Warner Bros. and the formation of Blackened Records, distributed by Rhino in the U.S. and Universal in the rest of the world. First product out of the gate would be *Quebec Magnetic*, a live DVD set that celebrates the band's relationship with the Canadian province of Quebec, which, lore has had it, accounts for 50 percent of all heavy metal

Right: Hammett's monster memorabilia was displayed at Kirk Von Hammett's Fear FestEvil at Grand Regency Ballroom on February 8, 2014, in San Francisco. *Steve Jennings/WireImage*

Below: Colisée Pepsi, Quebec City, Quebec, September 14, 2015. *Jeff Yeager/Michael Ochs Archives/Getty Images*

Rock in Rio, Rio de Janeiro, September 20, 2013. *Yasuyoshi Chiba/AFP/Getty Images*

Metallica: Through the Never was the 3D horror movie featuring live concert footage. *All Voyageur Press collection*

sales across Canada. The three hours of material includes covers of Bob Seger's "Turn the Page," Budgie's "Breadfan," and most obscurely, "Killing Time" from Sweet Savage, Vivian Campbell's NWO(Irish)HM band before the axeman's fame and accomplishments as part of the classic Dio lineup.

In September 2013, Metallica launched *Metallica: Through the Never*, the innovative 3D, no-dialogue horror movie marbled with Metallica live footage that Lars had been telling folks about at Orion. The soundtrack album to the movie, with its die-cut foldout presentation, was nominated for a Best Recording Packaging Grammy but didn't win—conversely, *Death Magnetic* had scooped up this award back in 2009. But Metallica would be on hand at the January 2014 awards ceremony nonetheless, reprising their first appearance at the soirée in '92 when they played "One," this time working their way through the epic antiwar anthem along with pianist Lang Lang.

James framed the Orion fest as a "financial disaster," and *Through the Never* didn't fare much better, getting nowhere close to recouping its $32 million budget. "I really, really thought that we made a really, really great movie," mused Kirk, again speaking with Stereogum. "I'll be very blunt about it. We put so much time and so much effort and made sure it was exactly the way that we envisioned it. Our fans definitely went to movie theaters

Pianist Lang Lang performs "One" with Metallica at the fifty-sixth annual Grammy Awards, Staples Center, Los Angeles, January 26, 2014. *Francis Specker/CBS via Getty Images*

BOGOTÁ, COLOMBIA

Metallica by Request Tour, Estadio Único de la Plata, La Plata, Argentina, March 29, 2014. Grupo 13/LatinContent/Getty Images

Inset: The downloadable album art for the digital Metallica by Request date at Parque Simón Bolívar, Bogotá, Colombia, March 16, 2014. Voyageur Press collection

Above: Metallica becomes the first band to play all seven continents with a performance at Argentina's Carlini Base, Antarctica, on December 8, 2013. The small and chilly but sunny show resulted in the digital live album *Freeze 'Em All. STR/AFP/Getty Images*

Both Voyageur Press collection

and saw the film, but the people that we were counting on to buy movie tickets—which was your casual moviegoer—they weren't as motivated to buy a ticket as our fans. For us, that was a big question mark. Why? We couldn't figure it out. We know we made a great movie and we felt good about it, but now it's time for us to move onto our next thing."

On December 8, 2013, that next thing turned out to be a gig in Antarctica, making Metallica the first band to have performed on all seven continents—the intimate, chilly but sunny show generated a digital live album called *Freeze 'Em All*. Further innovations on the live front included a stand at the decidedly non-metal Glastonbury

as well as the Metallica by Request tour. Along the way, we got a new Metallica song called "Lords of Summer" and sporadic, if regular, tour dates, including BlizzCon 2014, Lollapalooza 2015, and campaigns to Europe and South America. May 2, 2015, brought the band to their third annual Metallica Day concert at AT&T Park in hometown San Francisco, and six weeks later, Kirk and James knocked off "The Star-Spangled Banner" on electric guitar at an across-the-bay NBA playoff game between the Golden State Warriors and the Cleveland Cavaliers.

"Of course, the Metallica family around the world is loud and proud and knows the songs," reflected James,

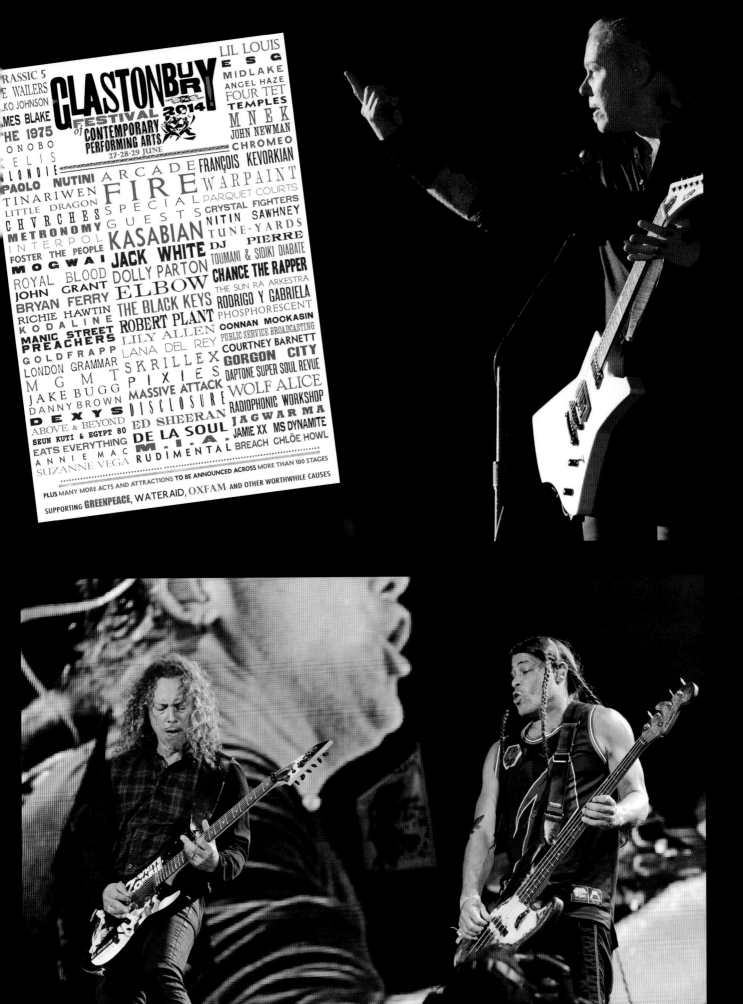

Top: Glastonbury Festival of Music and Performing Arts, Somerset, England, June 28, 2014. *Leon Neal/AFP/Getty Images*
Inset: Glastonbury 2014 poster. Metallica was announced as a headliner after the initial lineup was named and so did not appear on this piece. *Voyageur Press collection*
Bottom: Glastonbury Festival of Music and Performing Arts, Somerset, England, June 28, 2014. *Brian Rasic/Getty Images*

"Lords of Summer" single, 2014. *Voyageur Press collection*

Heavy Montreal Festival, Montreal, Quebec, August 9, 2014. *Mark Horton/ Getty Images*

speaking with Hitradio Ö3 on life as a live performer into his fifties. "If I happen to forget one of the words, they're there to help me out [laughs]. I don't know, I expect that people are there to give their energy. Because we give our energy, they give back, and we feed off of the energy. Sometimes it takes a few songs to get that going, or sometimes it's there right off the intro tape. So we don't expect anything, really. We're there to perform. And people react the way they're supposed to react. You cannot control anything that happens out there. We're up there playing music, and however they celebrate that night is up to them."

But all along the way, despite the euphoria of live shows, Metallica has never forgotten that they have to make new records, even if with these four guys, it seems

to be returns in widening arcs, sessions started and interrupted, time flying by.

"We do have a lot of musical ideas," related Kirk to MTV.com in the summer of 2013. "We have something called the 'Riff Bank,' and the Riff Bank keeps getting bigger and bigger, still, to this day [laughs]. I'm writing stuff, Rob's writing stuff, James is writing stuff, Lars is writing stuff, continually expanding the Riff Bank. So, it doesn't look like we're going to be putting out an album any time soon this year; it would be an amazing stroke of luck and grace if our album came out next year. I think it's a more sober statement to make to say that the album will probably come out in 2015. That's a sober, realistic thing; but we're psyched about it. It's too early in the game to tell you it will sound like *Death Magnetic*. I mean, we have

Lollapalooza, Grant Park, Chicago, August 1, 2015. *Gary Miller/FilmMagic*

The Veterans Day Concert for Valor on the National Mall, Washington, D.C., November 11, 2014.
Ricky Carioti/The Washington Post via Getty Images

a lot of ideas but no actual finished songs, so it's hard for me to give you an accurate description. But we're looking forward to making it as heavy and as high energy as possible, because that's what we want."

As 2015 came to an end, word had it that Metallica was in recording mode once again, although the fans have been conditioned to realize that with a ship this big, arrival at the dock takes a while—after all, this is a band that has delivered only four studio albums in the past twenty years, while, granted, never seeming to be retired or semi-retired. In fact, James, Kirk, Lars, and Robert never seem far from view, headbanging along with the fan base in one way or another, new album be damned.

Indeed, if it's not a massive live album, a birthday party for Lemmy, a record with Lou Reed, or a classical album, it's something even more unexpected—and increasingly so. We've now

Both Voyageur Press collection

Rock in Rio USA, MGM Resorts Festival Grounds, Las Vegas, Nevada, May 8, 2015. *Christopher Polk/Getty Images*

Sonisphere Festival, Milan, Italy, June 2, 2015. *Jeff Yeager/
Michael Ochs Archives/Getty Images*

Sonisphere Festival, Milan, Italy, June 2, 2015. *Francesco Castaldo/
Pacific Press/LightRocket via Getty Images*

192

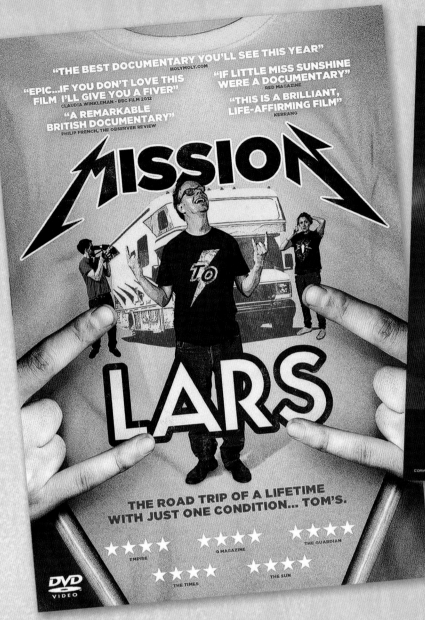

Voyageur Press collection

Above: The 2012 documentary *Mission to Lars* concerns an English fan with Fragile X syndrome and his family's efforts to help him meet Ulrich at a gig in 2009. Spoiler alert: he succeeds.
Voyageur Press collection

Below: Metallica beer was produced in conjunction with, fittingly, working-man's brand Budweiser.
Courtesy Anheuser-Busch InBev

had a limited-edition Metallica beer (in conjunction, fittingly, with working-man's brand Budweiser); there's been a second recent Metallica-themed film in the touching *Mission to Lars*; and the band's muso bassist Robert Trujillo, along with his eldest son John Pastorius IV, has just produced a documentary on bass legend Jaco Pastorius.

Yet still, on the subject of when—or how or why—Metallica one day ends, James proposes, "Why? It stops because . . . well, death doesn't stop it, pyrotechnics don't stop it, people leaving don't stop it. Yeah, what does stop it? Bus accidents, all that . . . I don't know. I think when Lars and I decide to not do it or we don't feel it

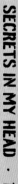

Rock in Rio, Rio de Janeiro, Brazil, September 19, 2015. *Raphael Dias/Getty Images*

Above: Orion Music + More Festival, Belle Isle Park, Detroit, June 9, 2013. *Scott Legato/Getty Images*

or something happens to one of us, then it probably stops. But that doesn't mean the spirit of Metallica or the love for it stops. Writing music will always be a part of me and my expression. Being on stage, I feel bipolar up there. I go from just mean, crazy monster to 'Nothing Else Matters,' where I'm trying to reach into people's souls and connect. So there are a lot of extremes up there, and depending on the song, it takes you there."

And is there finally a full-on sense of satisfaction, of accomplishment? "Absolutely. It's getting more and more. It's easier to do that. Possibly tonight when you see us on stage . . . it's all goofy, seeing four guys smile so much, but it feels good to be up there and really know that this is why we were put on Earth, I believe, to be together and to create music and create a fun live show where people can let loose."

SELECTED DISCOGRAPHY

A few notes on this discography. This is a U.S. discography, with U.S. chart placements and U.S. certifications, which weeds out myriad permutations that would turn this into a book itself. The singles discography is a little different, however. Given that in Metallica's case, this is a rubric of international and U.S. singles—7-inches, 12-inches, quasi-EPs, cassette singles, CD singles, variants everywhere, and many, many promos—I've decided to list one item only, prioritizing as: commercial U.S. singles, then promo U.S. singles, and then, if neither exist, key definable foreign issues, most notably U.K. product from the early days. Some foreign issue–only situations I've skipped, cause this was really only to give props to those early Music for Nations items. Call this a selected singles discography, if you must. Its use, one supposes, is in demonstrating which tracks from each album the band was proposing as singles.

Anyway, back to albums for this definite album band (and that's always a compliment in my books), Side 1 and Side 2 designations are provided for everything up to . . And Justice for All, which would be the last Metallica album before the pronounced shift from LP to CD. Where possible, I've endeavored to reduce repetition (i.e., for live albums that were issued both in audio and video format). Catalog numbers and other descriptors are for the first U.S. issue/instance of any given title. The first edition, so to speak.

Summing up, the general idea was to limit this to the core, relevant discography (and, yes, videography, although detail is reduced here) due to space restrictions and also diminished returns in terms of interest level and sheer readability. Also, I've skipped chart placement for videos and DVDs. I figure the only chart measure that carries significance enough to mention is the actual Billboard 200 for albums. Nothing else matters.

STUDIO ALBUMS

KILL 'EM ALL
Label: Megaforce
Catalog No.: MRI 069
Release: July 25, 1983
Peak U.S. *Billboard*: No. 120
U.S. RIAA certification: 3x platinum
Producer: Paul Curcio

SIDE 1: 1. Hit the Lights 4:17; 2. The Four Horsemen 7:08; 3. Motorbreath 3:03; 4. Jump in the Fire 4:50; 5. (Anesthesia)–Pulling Teeth 3:27; 6. Whiplash 4:06
SIDE 2: 1. Phantom Lord 4:52; 2. No Remorse 6:24; 3. Seek & Destroy 6:50; 4. Metal Militia 6:06
Notes: James Hetfield: rhythm guitar/vocals; Kirk Hammett: lead guitar; Cliff Burton: bass; Lars Ulrich: drums.

RIDE THE LIGHTNING
Label: Megaforce
Catalog No.: MRI 769
Release: July 27, 1984
Peak U.S. *Billboard*: No. 100
U.S. RIAA certification: 6x platinum
Producer: Metallica

SIDE 1: 1. Fight Fire with Fire 4:44; 2. Ride the Lightning 6:36; 3. For Whom the Bell Tolls 5:10; 4. Fade to Black 6:56
SIDE 2: 1. Trapped Under Ice 4:03; Escape 4:23; 3. Creeping Death 6:36; 4. The Call of Ktulu 8:52
Note: Only briefly a Megaforce issue in the U.S., most copies being Elektra (60396).

MASTER OF PUPPETS
Label: Elektra
Catalog No.: 9 60439
Release: March 3, 1986
Peak U.S. *Billboard*: No. 29
U.S. RIAA certification: 6x platinum
Producers: Metallica and Flemming Rasmussen

SIDE 1: 1. Battery 5:12; 2. Master of Puppets 8:36; 3. The Thing That Should Not Be 6:37; 4. Welcome Home (Sanitarium) 6:27

SIDE 2: 1. Disposable Heroes 8:16; 2. Leper Messiah 5:40; 3. Orion 8:27; 4. Damage, Inc. 5:30

. . . AND JUSTICE FOR ALL

Label: Elektra

Catalog No.: 60812

Release: August 25, 1988

Peak U.S. *Billboard*: No. 6

U.S. RIAA certification: 8x platinum

Producers: Metallica with Flemming Rasmussen

SIDE 1: 1. Blackened 6:40; 2. . . . And Justice for All 9:44

SIDE 2: 1. Eye of the Beholder 6:25; 2. One 7:24

SIDE 3: 1. The Shortest Straw 6:35; 2. The Frayed Ends of Sanity 7:40

SIDE 4: 1. To Live Is to Die 9:48; 2. Dyers Eve 5:12

Note: Bassist Jason Newsted replaces deceased Cliff Burton.

METALLICA

Label: Elektra

Catalog No.: 61113

Release: August 13, 1991

Peak U.S. *Billboard*: No. 1

U.S. RIAA certification: 16x platinum

Producers: Bob Rock with James Hetfield and Lars Ulrich

1. Enter Sandman 5:31; 2. Sad but True 5:24; 3. Holier Than Thou 3:47; 4. The Unforgiven 6:27; 5. Wherever I May Roam 6:44; 6. Don't Tread on Me 4:00; 7. Through the Never 4:04; 8. Nothing Else Matters 6:28; 9. Of Wolf and Man 4:16 10. The God That Failed 5:08; 11. My Friend of Misery 6:49; 12. The Struggle Within 3:53

LOAD

Label: Elektra

Catalog No.: 61923

Release: June 4, 1996

Peak U.S. *Billboard*: No. 1

U.S. RIAA certification: 5x platinum

Producers: Bob Rock with James Hetfield and Lars Ulrich

1. Ain't My Bitch 5:04; 2. 2 X 4 5:28; 3. The House That Jack Built 6:39; 4. Until It Sleeps 4:30; 5. King Nothing 5:28; 6. Hero of the Day 4:22; 7. Bleeding Me 8:18; 8. Cure 4:54; 9. Poor Twisted Me 4:00; 10. "Wasting My Hate" 3:57; 11. Mama Said 5:19; 12. Thorn Within 5:51; 13. Ronnie 5:17; 14. The Outlaw Torn 9:53

RELOAD

Label: Elektra

Catalog No.: 62126

Release: November 18, 1997

Peak U.S. *Billboard*: No. 1

U.S. RIAA certification: 4x platinum

Producers: Bob Rock with James Hetfield and Lars Ulrich

1. Fuel 4:29; 2. The Memory Remains 4:39; 3. Devil's Dance 5:18; 4. The Unforgiven II 6:36; 5. Better Than You 5:21; 6. Slither 5:13; 7. Carpe Diem Baby 6:12; 8. Bad Seed 4:05; 9. Where the Wild Things Are 6:54; 10. Prince Charming 6:05; 11. Low Man's Lyric 7:36; 12. Attitude 5:16; 13. Fixxxer 8:15

ST. ANGER

Label: Elektra

Catalog No.: 62853

Release: June 5, 2003

Peak U.S. *Billboard*: No. 1

U.S. RIAA certification: 2x platinum

Producers: Bob Rock and Metallica

CD: 1. Frantic 5:50; 2. St. Anger 7:21; 3. Some Kind of Monster 8:26; 4. Dirty Window 5:25; 5. Invisible Kid 8:30; 6. My World 5:46; 7. Shoot Me Again 7:10; 8. Sweet Amber 5:27; 9. The Unnamed Feeling 7:10; 10. Purify 5:14; 11. All Within My Hands 8:48

DVD: 1. Frantic 6:42; 2. St. Anger 7:40; 3. Some Kind of Monster 8:41; 4. Dirty Window 6:22; 5. Invisible Kid 8:54; 6. My World 6:09; 7. Shoot Me Again 7:24; 8. Sweet Amber 5:54; 9. The Unnamed Feeling 7:37; 10. Purify 5:29; 11. All Within My Hands 9:36

Notes: Bassist Bob Rock replaces Jason Newsted (nonofficial band member, studio only). CD also includes Metallica Video Game Preview (0:45). DVD consists of rehearsal versions all the CD songs, sequenced in the same order. New official member Robert Trujillo is bassist on rehearsal DVD.

DEATH MAGNETIC

Label: Warner Bros.

Catalog No.: 508732

Release: September 12, 2008

Peak U.S. *Billboard*: No. 1

U.S. RIAA certification: 2x platinum

Producer: Rick Rubin

1. That Was Just Your Life 7:08; 2. The End of the Line 7:52; 3. Broken, Beat & Scarred 6:25; 4. The Day That Never Comes 7:56; 5. All Nightmare Long 7:58; 6. Cyanide 6:39; 7. The Unforgiven III 7:46; 8. The Judas Kiss 8:00; 9. Suicide & Redemption 9:57; 10. My Apocalypse 5:01

Note: Bassist Robert Trujillo replaces Bob Rock.

LIVE ALBUMS

LIVE SHIT: BINGE & PURGE

Label: Elektra
Catalog No.: 61594
Release: November 23, 1993
Peak U.S. *Billboard*: No. 26
U.S. RIAA certification: 15x platinum
Producers: James Hetfield and Lars Ulrich

CD1: 1. The Ecstasy of Gold/Enter Sandman 7:28; 2. Creeping Death 7:28; 3. Harvester of Sorrow 7:19; 4. Welcome Home (Sanitarium) 6:39; 5. Sad but True 6:07; 6. Of Wolf and Man 6:22; 7. The Unforgiven 6:48; 8. Justice Medley 9:38; 9. Solos 18:49

CD2: 1. Through the Never 3:47; 2. For Whom the Bell Tolls 5:48; 3. Fade to Black 7:12; 4. Master of Puppets 4:35; 5. Seek & Destroy 18:08; 6. Whiplash 5:34

CD3: 1. Nothing Else Matters 6:03; 2. Wherever I May Roam 6:33; 3. Am I Evil? 5:42; 4. Last Caress 1:25; 5. One 10:27; 6. So What/Battery 10:05; 7. The Four Horsemen 6:08; 8. Motorbreath 3:14; 9. Stone Cold Crazy 5:32

VHS1: 1. 20 Min. MetalliMovie; 2. The Ecstasy of Gold; 3. Enter Sandman; 4. Creeping Death; 5. Harvester of Sorrow; 6. Welcome Home (Sanitarium); 7. Sad but True; 8. Wherever I May Roam; 9. Bass Solo; 10. Through the Never; 11. The Unforgiven; 12. Justice Medley; 13. Drum Solo and Drum Battle; 14. Guitar Solo;

VHS2: 1. The Four Horsemen; 2. For Whom the Bell Tolls; 3. Fade to Black; 4. Whiplash; 5. Master of Puppets; 6. Seek & Destroy; 7. One; 8. Last Caress; 9. Am I Evil?; 10. Battery; 11. Stone Cold Crazy

VHS3: 1. The Ecstasy of Gold; 2. Blackened; 3. For Whom the Bell Tolls; 4. Welcome Home (Sanitarium); 5. Harvester of Sorrow; 6. The Four Horsemen; 7. The Thing That Should Not Be; 8. Bass Solo; 9. Master of Puppets; 10. Fade to Black; 11. Seek & Destroy; 12. . . .And Justice for All; 13. One; 14. Creeping Death; 15. Guitar Solo; 16. Battery; 17. Last Caress; 18. Am I Evil?; 19. Whiplash; 20. Breadfan

Notes: The three VHS tapes from the original issue were converted to two DVDs for the reissue. VH1 and VH2 recorded in San Diego; VHS3 in Seattle.

S&M

Label: Elektra
Catalog: 62463
Release: November 23, 1999
U.S. *Billboard*: No. 182
U.S. RIAA certification: 5x platinum
Producers: Bob Rock with James Hetfield and Lars Ulrich, and Michael Kamen

CD1: 1. The Ecstasy of Gold 2:31; 2. The Call of Ktulu 9:34; 3. Master of Puppets 8:55; 4. Of Wolf and Man 4:19; 5. The Thing That Should Not Be 7:27; 6. Fuel 4:36; 7. The Memory Remains 4:42; 8. No Leaf Clover 5:43; 9. Hero of the Day 4:45; 10. Devil's Dance 5:26; 11. Bleeding Me 9:02

CD2: 1. Nothing Else Matters 6:47; 2. Until It Sleeps 4:30; 3. For Whom the Bell Tolls 4:52; 4. – Human 4:20; 5. Wherever I May Roam 7:02; 6. The Outlaw Torn 9:59; 7. Sad but True 5:46; 8. One 7:53; 9. Enter Sandman 7:39; 10. Battery 7:25

Note: Live album with the San Francisco Symphony.

METALLICA: THROUGH THE NEVER

Label: Blackened Recordings
Catalog No.: BLCKND021-2
Release: September 24, 2013
Peak U.S. *Billboard*: No. 9
U.S. RIAA certification: n/a
Producer: Greg Fidelman

CD1: 1. The Ecstasy of Gold 2:01; 2. Creeping Death 6:19; 3. For Whom the Bell Tolls 4:40; 4. Fuel 3:57; 5. Ride the Lightning 6:54; 6. One 8:25; 7. The Memory Remains 5:43; 8. Wherever I May Roam 6:16

CD2: 1. Cyanide 7:01; 2. . . . And Justice for All 9:16; 3. Master of Puppets 8:25; 4. Battery 5:12; 5. Nothing Else Matters 7:22; 6. Enter Sandman 6:19; 7. Hit the Lights 4:40; Orion 8:26

Note: Considered a soundtrack album to the film, this is indeed a standard live album, capturing the band recorded live at Rexall Place, Edmonton, Alberta, on August 17 and 18, 2012, and Rogers Arena, Vancouver, British Columbia, on August 24, 25, and 27, 2012.

MISCELLANEOUS AUDIO RELEASES

THE $5.98 EP: GARAGE DAYS RE-REVISITED
Label: Elektra
Catalog: 60757
Release: August 21, 1987
U.S. *Billboard*: No. 28
U.S. RIAA certification: Platinum
Producers: Metallica

SIDE 1: 1. Helpless (Diamond Head) 6:36; 2. The Small Hours (Holocaust) 6:39
SIDE 2: 1. The Wait (Killing Joke) 4:55; 2. Crash Course in Brain Surgery (Budgie) 3:10; 3. Last Caress/Green Hell (the Misfits) 3:28
Note: Covers EP; original artists noted in parentheses.

GARAGE INC.
Label: Elektra
Catalog: 62299
Release: November 24, 1998
U.S. *Billboard*: No. 2
U.S. RIAA certification: 5x platinum
Producers: Bob Rock with James Hetfield and Lars Ulrich

CD1: 1. Free Speech for the Dumb (Discharge) 2:35; 2. It's Electric (Diamond Head) 3:33; 3. Sabra Cadabra (Black Sabbath) 6:20; 4. Turn the Page (Bob Seger) 6:06; 5. Die, Die My Darling (the Misfits) 2:29; 6. Loverman (Nick Cave and the Bad Seeds) 7:52; 7. Mercyful Fate (Mercyful Fate) 11:11; 8. Astronomy (Blue Öyster Cult) 6:37; 9. Whiskey in the Jar (Trad., inspired by Thin Lizzy version) 5:04; 10. Tuesday's Gone (Lynyrd Skynyrd) 9:05; 11. The More I See (Discharge) 4:48
CD2: 1. Helpless (Diamond Head) 6:38; 2. The Small Hours (Holocaust) 6:43; 3. The Wait (Killing Joke) 4:55; 4. Crash Course in Brain Surgery (Budgie) 3:10; 5. Last Caress/Green Hell (the Misfits) 3:29; 6. Am I Evil? (Diamond Head) 7:50; 7. Blitzkrieg (Blitzkrieg) 3:36; 8. Breadfan (Budgie) 5:41; 9. The Prince (Diamond Head) 4:25; 10. Stone Cold Crazy (Queen) 2:17; 11. So What (Anti-Nowhere League) 3:08; 12. Killing Time (Sweet Savage) 3:03; 13. Overkill (Motörhead) 4:04; 14. Damage Case (Motörhead) 3:40; 15. Stone Dead Forever (Motörhead) 4:51; 16. Too Late Too Late (Motörhead) 3:12
Note: Compilation of Metallica covers so far, plus new recordings of covers; original artists noted in parentheses.

LULU
Label: Warner Bros.
Catalog: 529084
Release: October 31, 2011
U.S. *Billboard*: No. 36
U.S. RIAA certification: none
Producers: Lou Reed, Metallica, Hal Willner, and Greg Fidelman

CD1: 1. Brandenburg Gate 4:19; 2. The View 5:17; 3. Pumping Blood 7:24; 4. Mistress Dead 6:51; 5. Iced Honey 4:36
CD2: 1. Frustration 8:34; 2. Little Dog 8:01; 3. Dragon 11:08; 4. Junior Dad 19:29
Note: Studio collaboration with Lou Reed.

BEYOND MAGNETIC
Label: Warner Bros.
Catalog: 530093
Release: January 30, 2012
U.S. *Billboard*: No. 29
U.S. RIAA certification: None
Producer: Rick Rubin

1. Hate Train 6:59; 2. Just a Bullet Away 7:11; 3. Hell and Back 6:57; 4. Rebel of Babylon 8:01
Note: Listing above is for first physical issue, as CD EP, but initial issue was as download, on December 13, 2011.

SINGLES

Whiplash (Special Neckbrace Remix) b/w Jump in the Fire/Seek & Destroy (Live)/Phantom Lord (Live); Megaforce MRS-04

Jump in the Fire b/w Seek & Destroy (Live)/Phantom Lord (Live); Music for Nations KUT 105; various formats in European countries

Fade to Black (Vocal/LP Version) b/w Fade to Black (Vocal/LP Version); U.S. Elektra ED 5044 promo, plus green-vinyl U.K. promo

Creeping Death b/w Am I Evil/Blitzkrieg; Music for Nations KUT 112; also in picture disc version

For Whom the Bell Tolls (Edit) with For Whom the Bell Tolls; US Elektra ED 5026 promo

Master of Puppets (Part 1) b/w Master of Puppets (Part 1); U.S. Elektra ED 5139 promo; also officially released in France as a single by Music for Nations b/w Welcome Home Sanitarium

Harvester of Sorrow b/w Breadfan/The Prince; European issue, primarily U.K. Vertigo Metal 212/870614; issued in CD and 12-inch format plus a 7-inch promo

Eye of the Beholder b/w Breadfan; Elektra 7-69357, also in U.S. as CD promo and cassette single

. . . And Justice for All (Edit) b/w . . . And Justice for All (LP version); Elektra ED 5396 promo; also as CD promo

One b/w The Prince; Elektra 7-69329; issued worldwide in a variety of formats and track list variations

Enter Sandman; Elektra PRCD 8407-2 promo; issued commercially in Europe in variety of formats and commercially in U.S. as cassette single

Don't Tread on Me; Elektra PRCD 8728-2 promo

The Unforgiven (LP version); Elektra PRCD 8478-2 promo; issued commercially in Europe in variety of formats

Nothing Else Matters (Edit); Elektra PRCD 8534-2 promo; issued commercially in Europe in variety of formats and commercially in U.S. as cassette single

Wherever I May Roam (Edit); Elektra PRCD 8592-2 promo; issued commercially in Europe in variety of formats and commercially in U.S. as cassette single

Sad but True b/w So What; Elektra 4-64696; U.S. issue is cassette single

Until It Sleeps b/w Overkill; Elektra 64276-2

Hero of the Day b/w Kill/Ride Medley (Live); Elektra 64248-2

King Nothing b/w Ain't My Bitch (Live); Elektra 64197-2

Bleeding Me (Edited Version) b/w Bleeding Me (Full Version); Elektra PRCD 9820-2 promo

The Memory Remains b/w For Whom the Bell Tolls (Haven't Heart It Yet Mix); Elektra 64126-2

The Unforgiven II b/w The Thing That Should Not Be (Live); Elektra 64114-2

Better Than You; Elektra PRCD 1149-2 promo

Fuel; Elektra PRCD 1106-2 promo

Turn the Page (Edit) b/w Turn the Page (Album Version); Elektra PRCD 1226-2 promo

Whiskey in the Jar (Edit) b/w Whiskey in the Jar (Album Version); Elektra PRCD 1247-2 promo

Die, Die My Darling; Elektra PRCD 1314-2 promo

No Leaf Clover; Elektra PRCD 1430-2 promo

Hero of the Day (Live); Elektra PRCD 1465-2 promo

I Disappear; Hollywood PRCD-11243-2 promo

Frantic (Radio Edit) b/w Frantic (Album Version/Frantic (Live Version); Elektra PRCD 1913 promo

The Unnamed Feeling (Radio Edit) b/w The Unnamed Feeling (Album Version); Elektra PRCD 1948 promo

All Nightmare Long (Radio Edit); Warner Bros. PRO-CDR-520163 promo

VIDEOGRAPHY

CLIFF 'EM ALL $19.98 HOME VID
Label: Elektra
Catalog: 40106
Release: November 28, 1987
U.S. RIAA certification: 4x platinum
Note: VHS-only compilation of early live footage in tribute to recently deceased bassist Cliff Burton.

2 OF ONE
Label: Elektra
Catalog: 40109
Release: June 20, 1989
U.S. RIAA certification: 7x platinum
Note: Two versions of the video for "One," plus interview with Lars. VHS only.

A YEAR AND A HALF IN THE LIFE OF METALLICA

Label: Elektra
Catalog: 40148-3
Release: November 17, 1992
U.S. RIAA certification: 13x platinum
Notes: Documentary on the making of *Metallica*. Reissued on DVD in 1999.

LIVE SHIT: BINGE & PURGE

Label: Elektra
Catalog: 61594
Release: November 23, 1993
U.S. RIAA certification: 15x platinum
Notes: Combination audio and video product. Video originally released as VHS and later as DVDs (2002). Video footage is from San Diego and Seattle shows, while audio is from multiple Mexico City shows.

CUNNING STUNTS

Label: Elektra
Catalog: 40206
Release: December 8, 1998
U.S. RIAA certification: 3x platinum
Notes: Concert video from Fort Worth, Texas, May 9–10, 1997. Also issued as VHS.

S&M

Label: Elektra
Catalog: 40218
Release: November 23, 1999
U.S. RIAA certification: 6x platinum
Note: Video version of double-CD release (see above).

CLASSIC ALBUMS: METALLICA – METALLICA

Label: Eagle Vision
Catalog: EE 19001
Release: November 6, 2001
U.S. RIAA certification: Platinum
Note: The making of *Metallica*, from the popular series.

SOME KIND OF MONSTER

Label: Paramount Pictures
Release: January 25, 2005
U.S. RIAA certification: n/a
Note: Award-winning documentary on the turmoil surrounding the making of *St. Anger*.

THE VIDEOS 1989–2004

Label: Warner Bros.
Catalog No.: 38696
Release: December 4, 2006
U.S. RIAA certification: n/a

QUEBEC MAGNETIC

Label: Blackened Recordings
Catalog No.: BLCKND001
Release: December 11, 2012
U.S. RIAA certification: n/a
Notes: Concert video filmed in Quebec City, October 31–November 1, 2009. Blu-ray for the U.S. and Canada.

MUSIC VIDEOS

One, 1989; directed by Bill Pope and Michael Salomon
Enter Sandman, 1991; directed by Wayne Isham
The Unforgiven, 1991; directed by Matt Mahurin
Nothing Else Matters, 1992; directed by Adam Dubin
Wherever I May Roam, 1992; directed by Wayne Isham
Sad but True, 1992; directed by Wayne Isham
Until It Sleeps, 1996; directed by Samuel Bayer
Hero of the Day, 1996; directed by Anton Corbijn
Mama Said, 1996; directed by Anton Corbijn
King Nothing, 1997; directed by Matt Mahurin
The Memory Remains, 1997; directed by Paul Andresen
The Unforgiven II, 1998; directed by Matt Mahurin
Fuel, 1998; directed by Wayne Isham
Turn the Page, 1998; directed by Jonas Akerlund
Whiskey in the Jar, 1999; directed by Jonas Akerlund
No Leaf Clover, 1999; directed by Wayne Isham
I Disappear, 2000; directed by Wayne Isham
St. Anger, 2003; directed by The Malloys
Frantic, 2003; directed by Wayne Isham
The Unnamed Feeling, 2004; directed by The Malloys
Some Kind of Monster, 2004; directed by Bruce Sinofsky
The Day That Never Comes, 2008; directed by Peter Hjors and Thomas Vinterberg
All Nightmare Long, 2008; directed by Roboshobo
Broken, Beat & Scarred, 2009; directed by Wayne Isham
The View, (Metallica and Lou Reed) 2011; directed by Darren Aronofsky

INTERVIEWS
WITH THE AUTHOR

The lion's share of the quoted material in this book is sourced from personal interviews that I conducted, some multiple times with certain subjects. Participants in this Metalli-cause were: Michael Alago, Chuck Billy, Jim Florentine, Mike Fraser, Bill Hale, James Hetfield, Scott Ian, John Kornarens, Jason Newsted, Harald Oimoen, Ron Quintana, Brian Slagel, John Strednansky, Robert Trujillo, Lars Ulrich, and Jonny Zazula. Thanks to the above characters for their gracious participation and personal insights.

ADDITIONAL SOURCES

Bajus, Marilyn. "Ride the Lightning." *Metallion* 1, No. 3 (December 1984/January 1985).

Chirazi, Steffan. "Metallica: Thrash on Delivery." *Sounds*, February 15, 1986.

Doe, Bernard. "Metallica: Lightning Raiders." *Metal Forces* 8 (1984).

Elliott, Paul. "From Flotsam to Jetsam: The Reforging of Metallica." *Sounds*, February 7, 1987.

Epstein, Jon. "An Interview With: Lars Ulrich." *US Rocker* 2, No. 5 (April 1991).

Fisher, Kevin. "Ride the Lightning." *Grinder* 3 (1984).

Gundersen, Edna. "Metallica, Lou Reed Go on a Genre Bender with *Lulu*." *USA Today*, October 31, 2011.

Henderson, Tim. "Let's See If Anybody Buys This Crap!" *Brave Words & Bloody Knuckles* 72 (September 2003).

———. "Metallica." *M.E.A.T.* 25 (August 1991).

———. "The Waking of the Sandmen!" *Brave Words & Bloody Knuckles* 13 (June/July 1996).

Hetfield, James. Interview with Rock & Pop 95.9 FM, September 25, 2011.

"Metallica . . . And Justice for All!" *Brave Words & Bloody Knuckles* 5 (October/November 1994).

Hitradio Ö3. "Interview with James Hetfield." July 8, 2014.

Montgomery, James. "Metallica Planning a Withdrawal from 'The Riff Bank' for New Album." *MTV.com*. June 10, 2013.

Nalbandian, Bob. "Metallica: The Young Metal Attack." *The Headbanger 1* (1982).

Pratt, Greg. "Metallica: You Can't Hurt Me." Bravewords.com, 2008.

Rachel, T. Cole. "Q&A: Metallica's Kirk Hammett on the Launch of His New Horror Festival and What Lies Ahead for His Band." *Stereogum*. January 21, 2014.

Scott, Patrick, and **Bob Nalbandian.** "L.A. Metal Review: Metallica." *Metal Mania*, March 1982.

Secher, Andy. "Metallica: Thunder and Lightning." *Hit Parader* 265 (October 1986).

Turman, Katherine. "Metallica Album No. 6: *Load*." *Metal Hammer*, May 1996.

Welch, Chris. " . . . And Metallica for All." *Metal Hammer* 3, No. 11 (June 6, 1988).

ABOUT THE AUTHOR

Martin Popoff has been described as "the world's most famous heavy metal journalist." At approximately 7,900 (more than 7,000 appearing in his own books), he has unofficially written more record reviews than anybody in the history of music writing across all genres. Additionally, Martin has penned forty-two books on hard rock, heavy metal, classic rock, and record collecting. He was editor in chief of the now retired *Brave Words & Bloody Knuckles*, Canada's foremost metal publication for fourteen years, and has also contributed to *Revolver*, *Guitar World*, *Goldmine*, *Record Collector*, bravewords.com, lollipop.com, and hardradio.com, with many record label band bios and liner notes to his credit as well. Additionally, Martin worked for two years as researcher on the award-winning documentary *Rush: Beyond the Lighted Stage* and on *Metal Evolution*, an eleven-episode documentary series for VH1 Classic, and is the writer of the original metal genre chart used in *Metal: A Headbanger's Journey* and throughout the *Metal Evolution* episodes.

Born April 28, 1963, in Castlegar, British Columbia, and raised in nearby Trail, Martin went on to complete a BA and an MBA, work for Xerox, then co-own a graphic design and print-brokering firm before becoming a full-time rock critic in 1998. Gillan, Max Webster, Deep Purple, ZZ Top, and Black Sabbath are his favorite five bands of all time.

Martin currently resides in Toronto and can be reached through martinp@inforamp.net or www.martinpopoff.com. His website includes detailed descriptions and ordering information for the thirty or so books of his that are currently in print.

CONTRIBUTOR BIOS

Richard Bienstock is a senior editor with *Guitar World* magazine and the executive editor of *Guitar Aficionado* magazine, as well as the author of *Aerosmith: The Ultimate Illustrated History* (Voyageur Press). He is also a musician and journalist whose writings have appeared in numerous U.S. and international publications. He lives in Brooklyn, New York.

Daniel Bukszpan is the author of *The Encyclopedia of Heavy Metal*. He has been a freelance writer since 1994, and he has written for such publications as the *New York Post*, *Pop Smear*, *Guitar World*, the *Pit Report*, and *Hails and Horns*. He lives in Brooklyn with his wife, Asia, and his son, Roman.

Neil Daniels (www.neildaniels.com) has written about classic rock and heavy metal for a wide range of magazines, newspapers, fanzines, and websites. He is also the author of *Iron Maiden: The Ultimate Unauthorized History of the Beast* (Voyageur Press) and more than ten other books about artists, including Judas Priest, Robert Plant, Bon Jovi, Linkin Park, and Journey. He lives in Merseyside, England.

Andrew Earles (www.andrewearles.com) has written for *Vice*, *Spin*, *Magnet*, The Onion A/V Club, *Paste*, and *Decibel*, among other outlets since beginning his freelance career in 1999. The author of *Husker Du: The Story of the Noise-Pop Pioneers Who Invented Modern Rock* (Voyageur Press), Earles has contributed essays, reviews, and general creative content to ten other books. He lives in Memphis, Tennessee, with his wife and cat.

Kevin Estrada (kevinestrada.com) was a preteen when he began his photo career by smuggling his camera into some of the most legendary concerts in Los Angeles. For the last thirty-plus years he has photographed countless musicians in concert, backstage, on the road, and in the studio. He continues to make his living as a rock 'n' roll photographer and music video director in the L.A. area. He is blessed and supported by his wonderful wife and two beautiful daughters.

Gary Graff is co-author of *Neil Young: Long May You Run: The Illustrated History* and *Rock 'n' Roll Myths: The True Stories Behind the Most Infamous Legends*. He has also published books about Bruce Springsteen and Bob Seger and is the founding editor of the MusicHound Essential Album Guide series. In addition, he writes regularly for *Billboard*, the *New York Times* Features Syndicate, *Revolver*, and *Guitar Aficionado*, and he provides music coverage for WCSX in Detroit and WHQG in Milwaukee. Graff is based in Detroit, Rock City.

Bill Hale has been photographing rock bands since 1979. He is the former chief photographer of *Metal Rendezvous International* and the author of *Metallica: Club Dayz: 1982–1984*. He lives in Honolulu, Hawaii.

Bob Leafe (bobleafe.com) has photographed over fifteen hundred music performers, ranging from Led Zeppelin to Liberace. He has been the house photographer for major concert venues, radio stations, TV shows, and for MTV, where he shot their first Christmas video, the first Video Music Awards, and the 1984 New Year's Eve Ball. He's been published in more than one hundred U.S. magazines and all over the world.

Jaan Uhelszki was one of the founding editors at Detroit's legendary *CREEM* magazine. Her work has since appeared in *USA Today*, *Uncut*, *Rolling Stone*, *Spin*, *NME*, *Classic Rock*, *Guitar World*, and the *Braille Musician's Guide*. Currently she is the editor-at-large at *Relix* and the only journalist to have ever performed in full makeup with KISS.

Mick Wall (mickwall.com) is one of Britain's best-known music journalists, broadcasters, and authors. His book include the critically acclaimed biography of Metallica, *Enter Night* (2011). Formerly editor-in-chief of *Classic Rock* magazine and a founding father of *Kerrang!*, his work has also appeared in *The Times* (London), *Mojo*, *Guitar World*, and numerous other newspapers and magazines around the world. His thirty-five-year career has also included stints as a high-profile PR exec, artist manager, TV and radio presenter, and record company executive.

Frank White began his music photography career on February 12, 1975, shooting Led Zeppelin at Madison Square Garden. He started selling his photos to the public a year later and then to magazines in 1982—first to *Relix*, then to *Guitar World*, *Rock Fever*, *Circus*, *CREEM*, *Hit Parader*, *Rock Scene*, *Hard Rock*, *Rolling Stone*, and others. In 1986 he started Frank White Photo Agency, licensing his photos and those of others to record companies, book publishers, MTV, and later to VH1. That same year he became a touring photographer for bands and eventually traveled to England, Europe, and South America. In February 2010 he became a house photographer for The Iridium, a jazz and blues club in New York City. He continues to photograph artists and license photos worldwide.

INDEX

ACKNOWLEDGMENTS

Dennis Pernu; Tim Henderson; Kevin Estrada; Rich Galbraith; Bob Nalbandian; Vickie Strate; Jasonic; Brian Slagel; Deep Purple; the Banger Boys; Mom, Dad, and Brad; Beth and Trevor; and Metallica.

Quarto is the authority on a wide range of topics.

Quarto educates, entertains and enriches the lives of our readers—enthusiasts and lovers of hands-on living.

www.quartoknows.com

© 2013 Voyageur Press
Additional text and compilation © 2016 Quarto Publishing Group USA Inc.

First published in 2013 by Voyageur Press, an imprint of Quarto Publishing Group USA Inc., 400 First Avenue North, Suite 400, Minneapolis, MN 55401 USA. This edition published 2016. Telephone: (612) 344-8100 Fax: (612) 344-8692

quartoknows.com
Visit our blogs at quartoknows.com

Voyageur Press titles are also available at discounts in bulk quantity for industrial or sales-promotional use. For details contact the Special Sales Manager at Quarto Publishing Group USA Inc., 400 First Avenue North, Suite 400, Minneapolis, MN 55401 USA.

10 9 8 7 6 5 4 3 2 1

ISBN: 978-0-7603-5171-0

The Library of Congress has cataloged the first edition of this book as follows:

Popoff, Martin, 1963-
    Metallica : the complete illustrated history / Martin Popoff with Richard Bienstock [and eight others].
        pages cm
    Includes index.
    ISBN 978-0-7603-4482-8 (hc)
    1. Metallica (Musical group) 2. Rock musicians--United States--Biography. I. Bienstock, Richard. II. Title.
    ML421.M48P66 2013
    782.42166092'2--dc23
    [B]
                            2013005677

Acquiring Editor: Dennis Pernu
Art Director: James Kegley
Design: John Barnett
Layout: Simon Larkin

Printed in China